Life before the Taser

By: Douglas G. Barker

George:
Thanks for your
support. Enjoy the
book.

Doug

Published in 2012 by Douglas G. Barker

Library and Archives Canada Cataloguing in Publication

Barker, Douglas G., 1946-
    Life before the taser / by Douglas G. Barker.

ISBN 978-1-4699-5447-9

    1. Barker, Douglas G., 1946-. 2. Police--British Columbia--Vancouver--Biography. I. Title.

HV7911.B363A3 2012   363.2092   C2012-901400-1

Printed by CreateSpace

Dedication

To my Father who thought I was pretty funny and my Mother, who passed away while I was writing this book. It was she who partly inspired me to write it. One day she turned to me and out of the blue she said, "You've had quite an interesting life haven't you?"

Have you ever asked yourself, "How did Cops handle people before they implemented the Taser?"

The unruly jerk didn't just come about in the last 10 years, they have always been around and they were dealt with in the past without the use of the Taser.

I was at a shopping mall the other day and there was a uniformed policeman giving a traffic safety lecture to a group of senior citizens. The officer, about 5'7" tall was wearing on the outside of his police uniform shirt, a bullet proof vest equipped with an attached whistle, and a ball point pen. On the officers belt he was outfitted with a 9mm service pistol and two magazines or clips of extra ammunition, handcuffs, pepper spray, an Asp (a metal telescopic tactical baton), the Taser, a flash light and his police radio. Add to all this and he was wearing leather gloves for the lecture.

My wife looked at me and said," I thought this mall was safe" to which I replied "It is, but those seniors can get pretty violent at times."

After 26 years as a policeman in a large Canadian city I know how we got to this point of being heavily armed, but have we gone too far?

Preface

Life Before The Taser or getting cooperation the old fashioned
way, is the true story of a young man's career as a Vancouver
Police Officer from when he first decided to become a policeman
in 1975 as a naïve recruit, through years of experiences until his
retirement in 2001. The book describes the excitement, challenges
and disappointments an officer faces in a police career not to
mention the blunders and misdeeds that one might be remembered
for. The book will cover the job postings that the author worked in
where he relates many of the situations, both serious and funny, as
well as incidents that were not handled appropriately by the author.
There will be moments of fear, shock, violence and sometimes just
plain stupidity. The reader will learn that once you decide to
become a policeman you can say goodbye to some of your current
friends because not everyone likes a cop.

There was no shortage of interesting characters in the Vancouver
Police Force in the early 1970's from the Constable rank on up to
the Officers. This was an era where many of the older, more
senior members had 20 years or more of police service after having
been recruited just after World War II. I am told that just after the
war the city didn't have the funds to purchase uniforms for all the
new recruits so some recruits were sent out on patrol wearing a
Fedora hat, an overcoat and a shirt and tie until uniforms could be
purchased.

In 1975 when the author joined the police force the recruits were
issued uniforms unlike the late 1940's and their firearms were
better than the old .38 caliber Webley of the late 1940's and 50's
but the equipment issued was far inferior to what the street cop of
today gets issued. In the mid 1970's you were issued a six shot
.38 caliber Smith & Wesson revolver, 12 round nose bullets, a set
of hand cuffs and a rubber trudgen that only annoyed someone
when they were struck with it. Not only were there no Tasers in
1975, but neither were there bullet proof vests, pepper spray or
night sticks provided.

The incidents related in this book are not entirely uncommon during most police officers careers, but because of the author's work assignments, he has had more than his share of good stories. There are the typical police stories including violence, death, sex, booze and even police wrong doings but there is nothing about a Taser incident. The author is not overly proud of some of the events that occurred, but they happened and it wouldn't be the complete story if they were not told. The author does not give the conclusion to some of the police cases mentioned in the book but only his involvement in the case and what went right and what went wrong. The stories are true, the characters are real people however most but not all of the names have been changed in order to protect their identity.

While in New York City in October 2008, the author and his wife attended the David Letterman Show. While standing in line waiting to enter the theater, people were asked to write down a funny story they knew and the Letterman show may fly you back if they wanted to use it. The author completed the form with his police story and returned home to Vancouver the very next morning. When he returned home there was a phone message from the Letterman Show asking him if he was still in New York could he come by for a video audition. While the author never did get to appear on the show, the phone call from the show inspired him, because if they liked that story, he had many similar stories which he tells in this book.

Most people think of a police officer as a very serious person with no sense of humor. This is far from the truth. A sense of humor is a must if you want to make it to retirement.

The book was written after 10 years of retirement and hearing in the news of many cases of police shootings and what might be considered, by some, as the over-use of the Taser. The author shares some of his stories where a Taser might have been used if they were available at the time, but because they weren't available to the police, other forms of intervention were used, like old fashioned physical force or just talking, and negotiating, and using common sense.

The mid 1970's and early 80's was a different era and mindset than it is now. Many of the stories told in this book wouldn't take place now because of the current lack of manpower and the ever present cell phone camera carried by everyone to record all your police activities. There is a much greater call load now and probably not the down time to goof off as we sometimes did in the early days.

The book is essentially about police life before the Taser or as the author learns from some veteran colleagues, 95% common sense and 5% smarts.

The author struggled for years whether or not to write the book and tell his story knowing there will be some, police and civilians alike that will be offended by some of the events that occurred. There is good and bad in most stories and this one is no exception.

The opinions expressed in this book are those solely of the author and not necessarily those of the Vancouver Police Department or the past or current Vancouver Police Department members.

x

A New Career

It's a dreary, rainy morning in February 1975 and I am looking out the window from the top floor of the Marine Building where I have just opened an envelope containing a letter saying I am fired from my sales job at Dale & Co. Insurance. As I stare out to the Burrard Inlet and the North Shore Mountains I am pretty ticked off but not totally surprised. My job was as a commission salesman but I would receive a steady draw that would be repaid if my sales didn't equate to the draw amount. I had worked at a different company for 5 years and had done very well but I was wooed by Dale & Company to bring over my business and go after larger accounts. After working at Dale & Company for about 2 years it was not all that I expected it to be. I was able to bring over many accounts from the previous business but the large new accounts weren't as easy to pick up as I was told. Anyway, Dale & Company advise that I owe them $1200.00 for my draw account. They have been happy to keep the $700 per month business that I brought from my previous agency until now and will continue after I'm gone. The company president also wasn't happy that I separated from my wife of seven years a few months earlier. The president thought I wasn't paying enough attention to my work or my family. He was right, although I don't know that firing me resolved the problem; it just made it harder to pay support payments.

I was bored with my job and thought being fired is only one more rung of the ladder of life I have fallen from. It's a Friday and I am going home to have a drink and break the news to my room mates, not to mention my ex wife and my father who actually got me started in the insurance business and who I'm sure will be pretty disappointed with the news.

I read the newspaper that night knowing I have to find a job and I see an ad where the Vancouver Police Department is looking to hire 250 new police officers. The ad stated applicants must be at least 19 years of age, a Canadian Citizen, have a grade 12 education and be at least 5'9" and 150 pounds. I only had grade 11 and part of grade 12 as my school counselor thought it was best that I go and find a trade and quit school. Had I applied for the job a few years earlier grade 10 was the minimum requirement and 5'10" the minimum height.

I was playing rugby for the Kats Rugby Club at the time and there were some pretty tough guys there. I was no pansy but I wasn't the mean tough type either. I was in good shape, 28 years old, 5'11" 185 lbs and could run fast and for distance. As a rugby player you learned to play hurt as you were always suffering from some injury. It seemed I had a standing Doctors appointment every Monday after a Saturday game with a dislocated shoulder, missing teeth, dislocated fingers or broken toes. We practiced twice a week and played a game almost every Saturday except for the summer months. One of the guys upon hearing about my interest in police work said he didn't think I was tough enough to be a cop. I wondered if he was right. Then the same guy asked why I wanted to be a cop anyway? I didn't have an answer for him. I wasn't looking to help the needy or give back to my community, both very noble causes but usually done on a volunteer basis. I needed a paying job and this looked like it could be exciting.

I decided to put things in motion and see where they would lead so I applied for and got into a grade 12 equivalent course and passed. Then I went and got a photo of myself to attach to the employment application form. I wrote an exam with 100 other applicants at Sir Charles Tupper High School and found out a few weeks later that I failed the English portion of the exam. I re wrote the exam the next month and I was later told I passed the English but failed the math this time. The Staff Development Section did call me in for an interview with Inspector Ian MacGregor. Naturally I was dressed in a shirt and tie looking respectable and business like and he told me that I passed both subjects once so that was good enough for him. The Inspector walked me over to the window of his office and asked if I could read a neon sign that was half way down the block. I read the name to him and he seemed happy with that. He then asked if I had ever smoked marijuana and I thought ok, I'm in trouble. While I had, I hadn't very often as I was always too busy with a family and playing rugby so I was never into the hippy scene. I told the Inspector that I had tried it twice but never inhaled and didn't like it. I think President Bill Clinton stole my line. Inspector McGregor asked if I would take a polygraph exam on that question and I said I would. Then the Inspector asked if I would walk around the room. I guess he was looking for some poise and presence in my walk. He told me that I would be considered as a candidate but I would have to attend City Hall for a physical and attend at the Aquatic Centre for a swimming test. The Inspector said they would have to do a background check and that would take a while. I knew if I wanted to be a cop it was time to get a hair cut because the style of the time was long hair near your shoulders.

With my spirits lifted that I may get this job I continued to play rugby and collect unemployment insurance. I stopped looking for other work as I decided I really wanted this job. I hoped the back ground check would work out as I knew I had some skeletons in the closet.

I was an ordinary kid and a little shy at 13 years old. I never liked school and wasn't particularly interested in sports. My parents decided to send me to Saint Georges, a private school, for grade 7 for the extra help you would get in smaller classes. This worked and my marks in school improved and I became interested in sports and quite a good rugby player for my age. After completing grade 9 I transferred to Lord Byng High School and got interested in girls and started to act out. I was a good athlete playing rugby,

football, basketball and baseball but I was back to being a bad
student

We lived on the west side of Vancouver in the nice middle income
area of Point Grey. There were several kids I played sports with
whose fathers were policemen at the time. I thought that was neat
but it wasn't a big deal. The police department had gone through a
police corruption period in the early 1950's that largely centered
on Chief Constable Mulligan who later resigned and left town. My
baseball coach was Cliff Virtue who had been a motorcycle cop
and I played ball with Larry Mead whose father Cliff Mead was a
Police Inspector. In the next block was Terry Blythe whose father
was a policeman and Terry eventually became the Chief Constable
around 1997. These fathers all seemed to be nice ordinary guys
and I didn't have any fear of them nor was I in awe of their job. I
had no reason to be.

* * *

One summer night when I was 15 years old I made the mistake of
sleeping outside in our back yard tent so I could catch up with
these four other kids in the middle of the night. The plan was that
this other 15 year old kid, Glen, was going to borrow his Dad's car
and we would take it for a joy ride. Well we met him and started
driving around Vancouver around 3 in the morning. The problem
was in those days there were no all night gas stations and we were
almost out of gas. My father was right, when you start doing
something stupid it can just fester and get out of control and here I
am about to get out of control. We attempt to siphon gas from a
car in an open car port and things aren't going that well. It's
around 4 in the morning and it's getting a little lighter out. We see
a car about a block away driving towards us in the lane and the
smart kids scramble and take off. I decide to stay with Glen and
the car and sit in the front passenger seat. The car approaching us
turns out to be a police car with 2 policemen inside. It turns out
someone had phoned about some prowlers and we were them.
They split the two of us up and started questioning us. They didn't
know about the gas yet. I was sitting in the back of the police car

answering questions when they turn a spot light on to the garage and like the movie Stalag 17 there it is, brightly lit up, the cars gas tank with a hose leading down to an empty tub. The jig was up. The policeman in the back seat with me asked "Have you ever had trouble with the law." I replied "No, never." He asked again and again I said "no". I guess he didn't like the answer or perhaps I had a smart aleck tone because he cuffed me one with his open hand across my face. I think I began to cry and again I said "No I haven't."

There we were, now parked in front of my house in a nice part of town at 5 in the morning with the sun coming up and what looks like it will be a beautiful day. The two police officers walk me to the front door of my house and I ring the door bell hoping no one will answer. After a few minutes I say to one of them, "I guess no one's home; maybe you should take me downtown". With that the big guy pounds on the front door. My Mom and Dad both are there at the door dressed in their house coats and we go inside. The police tell the story and my Dad, the insurance salesman, says "great, I insure the cars and my kid steals them." That incident straightened me out forever because my parents were good decent people and I realized what my Dad meant about a small stupid prank festering into something greater.

* * *

Another concern about being accepted into the police was that I had my Drivers License suspended for a month seven years earlier because I had too many speeding tickets. It taught me a lesson because I hadn't had a speeding ticket since then and I hoped my new driving record would be accepted.

While I am waiting for the background checks to be completed I am hanging out at Kits Beach playing tennis and soaking up the sun. While I'm down there I meet 2 off duty policemen, Jimmy Yohimas, who happened to be the guy who gave me 3 of my speeding tickets years earlier causing me to have my license suspended and Bill Wellman who was a character in his own right. When they learned that I had applied for the job they gave me lots of coaching. Bill would sometimes come by my house on Point Grey Road with a few other motorcycle cops. Even though I had never ridden a motorcycle, other than a Moped, I thought that's what I wanted to do, be a motorcycle cop.

The back ground check had begun. I hadn't lived at home for 8 years and had worked for Woodward Stores, an Insurance Company, and Air Canada as a ramp rat or baggage handler and two Insurance Agencies. They also had to go and check out my schooling and talk with my counselor and talk to my neighbors. They talked to my separated wife and I guess she gave me an ok. They had to do a criminal records check and a Department of Motor Vehicle Licence check which would show my one month suspension.

I get called to attend City Hall and see the Police Department's Doctor. I am a specimen. Everything is good. I go into a hearing booth like the old TV show The 64 Thousand Dollar Question and have my hearing tested. Everything is ok. Then I have to look into a machine that checks my eye sight. There is a rubber mount that goes over both eyes at the same time as you look into the screen. The nurse asks me to close my right eye and look into the screen and tell her what I see. No Problem. The nurse then says close your left eye and tell her what I see with my right eye. I can't see a damn thing. Everything is very blurry. I'm not taking any chances here. I open my left eye and tell her what I see. She can't see I cheated using both eyes and I pass with 20/20 vision.

The next day I attend at the Aquatic Centre and do my swim. They would take you to the deep end at around 10 feet deep and have you dive from a floating position to retrieve a brick from the bottom. No Problem.

The process was getting close to being completed. I had been out with some of the guys at the liquor store picking up 100 cases of beer as we were having a big party at our house on the corner of Point Grey Road and McDonald. When we are unloading the beer into the house, Detective Fred Boyce from the Staff Development Section arrives. He and I sit down as the other guys move the beer around and he tells me about everyone he has talked to and as far as he is concerned I will be hired. Detective Boyce said, "Remember, the job is 95% common sense and 5% smarts". He even tried to recruit some of the guys from the house.

On July 2, 1975 I am sworn in by Deputy Chief Constable Tom Dixon. I am told to attend at the Department Supplies Store and pick up some equipment. While I don't get a uniform as I still have to attend the police academy, I do get a police badge, Badge # 276. The badge is still warm. I am told that the member that had this badge was fired this morning for sexual harassment. I am to start working as a Pre Recruit in the Hit and Run Squad starting the next Monday morning. At last, a pay cheque.

Back to school

In September 1975 I am assigned to the British Columbia Police Academy, class #3 which is being run out of some trailers at the Seaforth Armoury at 1st and Burrard. The British Columbia Police Academy is attended by all the municipal police forces in the province not just Vancouver. While Vancouver has the majority of members, there are classmates from Nelson, Victoria, Esquimalt, Saanich, Oakbay, West Vancouver and Port Moody. Upon arriving and looking around at the physical fitness of some of the other recruits I determine that yes, I should be tough enough to be a cop. Other than one fellow from Port Moody I am the oldest recruit at 29 where the majority of the classmates are in their early 20's. The course consists of 3 months at the academy, 3 months on the road with a training officer and then 3 months back at the academy. If you are lucky to get through all that then you will go out to the street for a year then back to the academy for a month and back to the street for another year and one more month at the Academy. After 3 years you will be considered a first class constable.

My concern goes back to my main problem; I hated school. I am going to have to work hard to get through the studies and memorization of law and traffic. I am an adult now and living in a rugby house with a bunch of rugby guys who are all working professionals and I have to be able to study on my own. One guy is a school teacher, one a marine biologist and one is the manager of a construction firm. They have done their schooling and are all quite successful, they don't care about me.

One night my girl friend at the time, Cari or Skinny Minni, as I affectionately called her, comes over to visit and I tell her I have to study and I can see her some other time. Well instead of leaving she goes down stairs to visit my room mates Clyde and Sean who are watching TV in the basement. I am trying to study and can't concentrate over the laughter and frivolity that is coming from the room beneath me. I go to the top of the stairs and ask them to keep the noise down as I am trying to study. It doesn't stop and I lose it. Besides the noise, maybe I was jealous that my girlfriend was downstairs with my room mates and I'm studying for an important law exam the next morning. Skinny Minni had left her purse up stairs and I took it and threw it out onto Point Grey Road. Then I threw a half empty coke bottle to the bottom of the stairs and walked down. I can tell you all eyes were wide open. I picked Skinny Minni up and threw her over my shoulder as if I were a fireman and carried her up the stairs to the main floor and escorted her to the front door and told her to leave. I was a real asshole but that's how much this job meant to me and I wasn't going to fail because of the studies. Skinny Minni and I always had an on and off relationship but we remain friends to this day.

When it came to the physical part I was comfortable, in fact I thrived on it. The long runs in the morning and the bare knuckle pushups in the parking lot on the cement. Some wimps would be cursing Bob Harling who was our PT instructor as we would be doing the push ups. This is what I expected. I loved it. Running from 1st avenue to Stanley Park and back and staying in shape. I was still going to rugby practice Tuesdays and Thursdays and playing on the weekends. One day Bob Harling says "Barker, get on the mat, (which is about 8 feet by 8 feet), with Lou Williams and Don Bestly. Barker, you are the bad guy and are to be arrested by the other two. Don't let it happen and don't leave the mat".

Lou Williams is 6'3" and 250lbs and Bestly is my size, 5'11" only a little soft like Jell-O. I knew there is no way I'm going to win this but I had to make it last as long as I can. I decide to go after Bestly and kick him and punch him in the head. While he is trying to figure out what happened I go after Lou Williams. We roll around on the mat and then Bestly gets back into action and the game is over. That is what it is about, surviving, trying your best and gathering a little courage.

* * *

One day at the Aquatic Centre we are instructed to jump off the 5 meter diving board. When you are on these boards they appear a lot higher than they are because you are actually looking at the bottom of the pool and not just the top of the water. A five meter diving board may only be about 15 feet but it looks like 26 feet. Some of the female members of the class were having difficulty jumping off the 5 meter board and I started to give them a hard time. To their credit they all eventually did jump. Bob Harling then said "who wants to jump off the 10 meter board". The females then said Barker does. I walked up to the top of the 10 meter board and looked down and my knees started to shake. It now looks like 41 feet and I realize I am afraid of heights. I am glad I didn't apply to be a fireman. One of the females yells," Hey Barker, don't you have any balls?" I decided I had to jump to save face, but I have to protect the very balls she was referring to. If the girls weren't there I probably would have walked back down to the 5 meter board but you have to do things sometimes you don't want to. I jumped and hit the water that felt like concrete. I bounced off the bottom of the pool pretty hard. I have no idea how the Olympic divers do it.

At the Academy we learned how to march, give first aid, shoot a hand gun as well as a shot gun and we learned how to drive a police car in a pursuit environment. I never was overly interested in guns before so this was a new experience in learning how to shoot, particularly under stress. The driving was something else. The driver training took place at the Boundary Bay Airport at an unused portion of an old runway. A course of slow and high speed corners were made up using cones and you were required to complete the course in a certain time with minimal cones being knocked over. There is a lot of adrenalin created when you put on the siren and start driving fast and the noise inside the car is unbelievable.

These were all exciting and subjects I didn't have much problem with. It was the studies and memorizing that was tough. Our Academy class was the third class of the year as the Department was trying to get the needed new 250 members as soon as possible. The class had about 40 members in it so we were split into two groups, class A and class B. The rush to find 250 new members in a short period of time turned out to be somewhat flawed as we lost about 25% of the students. At the end of every week someone would be called out in class and asked to take their books and go to the office. They would never be seen again. One of the victims was Don Bestly.

We completed block 1 of the training program and were now to be sent to our respective police departments for training in the field. We were all issued new uniforms, hats, shoes and guns. We were issued a Smith & Wesson 38 Caliber six shot revolver with 12 round nose bullets, our hand cuffs and the questionable rubber trudgen or Billy Club.

Now we were going to the real world and not the safety of the class simulations but we will be back at the Academy in 3 months if we are not killed or kicked out of the Force.

The Eye Opener

The City of Vancouver is broken up into 4 Districts with each District divided into areas known as Teams. Some Districts may have 6 Teams where another only 4. Each District has it own personality, traits and trouble spots. District One includes the downtown business district as well as the West End apartment area that has a lot of restaurants, night clubs, bars and movie theatres. District Two where the main police station and Headquarters is located contains The Downtown East Side sometimes referred to as Skid Row, Chinatown, the docks and commercial manufacturing as well as a large residential area. District Three has a lot of small commercial businesses, the Fraser River and a huge residential area. District Four is predominantly affluent residential with some commercial and the Vancouver beaches.

If you want to see some action you police in the Skids or Granville Mall and deal with the drunks and the druggies. If you want to write speeding tickets and get into car chases go to District Three or Four. If all you want to see are the beautiful people of Vancouver work in the District One downtown business core or District Four's beach area.

Each recruit from our class will be assigned two Districts to work in so we get a little variety on the type of calls we handle as well as the different types of people living in those Districts. We have no choice as to what District we will work in but we are told where we will work.

On my very first day I am assigned to work the afternoon shift in District one which is in the downtown West End. While I have a uniform I don't have a locker at the station so I have to wear my uniform from home. This shouldn't be a problem because everyone respects a police officer. Right! I am proud to be a policeman but I don't necessarily want everyone in the neighborhood to know what I do for a living. Anyway there I am all spiffed up on my way to my new career. I hope that I can fit in and not look too much like a dork on the first day. I have one thing in my favor at least, because I am 29 years old and not 19, I fit in the general age range of the other guys who are constables. It is a cold November day and the CFL Grey Cup football game is on TV in the parade room.

As a new recruit you are assigned to a field trainer who is supposed to be trained in assisting the recruit put his class knowledge to work on the road. This being 1975 it is the era of Disco Music, free love, pooka shells and long collar length hair for many of the younger policeman except me. I am assigned to Constable Stan Arthurs and he has the pooka shells, a necklace made of sea shells and the long collar length hair. This guy is about my age, a little smaller and has a pocked mark face. He isn't an overly attractive man. As we get into our police car Stan tells me "Don't touch anything kid until I tell you". I hadn't just fallen off a turnip truck and we were warned at the Academy to keep our eyes open and our mouths shut because there were trainers out there like this guy who wanted to impress a new recruit by showing what a great veteran they were.

We go for coffee at the Black Angus Restaurant at Thurlow and Davie and meet up with some of the other police members working the area. The West End of Vancouver is predominantly high rise apartments and a busy area. After coffee we drive around the area as Stan is showing me the turf. Stan asks me if I like jewelry and seeing all the gold chains and bracelets he's wearing I know what my answer should be. After saying yes, he takes me to a 'friend of his' that makes his own jewelry in an old garage. I meet the guy and I'm told anytime I want to buy jewelry, he will give me a good deal. I think to myself this seems pretty odd but I haven't put 2 and 2 together yet and want to keep my mouth shut. We get back in the car and continue to cruise the West End when Stan starts pointing out specific apartment buildings. "See that place there? I've got a girl that lives there". A few minutes later he would point out another place where one of his other girls lives. This happens a third time and I think bull shit. This guy is a mutt and he has girl friends all over the West End?

We are called over the police radio and the radio dispatcher requests that we return to headquarters. When we arrive at Headquarters I am told to see Sgt Jim Adem in his office. I think I haven't had time to do anything wrong so what's this about? The Sergeant tells me he is going to have me work with a different training officer and to get my belongings out of Constable Arthurs police car. I didn't mind a bit. As it turns out Arthurs was fired shortly after this. It seems the girls in the apartments were hookers that he helped look after and Internal Investigation had been watching Stan for sometime.

* * *

I am introduced to Constable Brian McClay. He is not a field trainer but his partner is on holidays and he has the respect of Sgt Adem to keep me out of trouble for a few weeks until a Field Trainer becomes available. McClay is about my age and stature and he has been on the job a couple of years. Unlike Stan, he appears normal and I am allowed to talk. Constable McClay is a beat man and we are going to walk the Granville Mall area in downtown Vancouver. Granville Street, in the downtown district is about 11 blocks long and would run all the way from Burrard Inlet to the north to False Creek to the south. Most of the trouble activity is going to be from the movie district to the Granville Bridge that crosses False Creek. We take a car from Headquarters and park it near Granville and get out on foot. When we were given our new uniforms we were only given a light navy blue uniform raincoat to wear over our tunics. All patrol members have a warm winter coat as this is, after all November, and a colder November than usual. The night was uneventful.

The next night, as Brian and I are walking our beat south on Granville Street, a marked police car pulls up and tells us to get in. The driver says there is a new club called the Gandy Dancer on Hamilton Street that they haven't been in before and he wants us to join them in checking it out. The four of us start to walk inside the premise as the senior officer talks to the door man and tells him the purpose of our visit and McClay and I walk by and inside the club. I have done some night clubbing and the place looks pretty nice. The music is really good and the place is packed, which is unusual for a Monday Night. I notice there are a lot of people dancing but I don't see many girls. Just when I figure out what this place is, a guy approaches me and says "Hi officer", in a wispy voice," do you want to dance?" I laughed and politely said no, that I was working. The guy persisted and asked if I would come back after my shift? At that point I told McClay I was getting out of there before I got kissed.

Walking the beat seemed pretty good and although I would only be doing it for a few weeks; it was probably not appropriate for a brand new recruit. Unlike the regular Patrol Units, you didn't get assigned many calls, calls like B&E reports that can take you off the road for some time. As a Beat Man you make your own cases as well as do a lot of public relations with business owners on the mall. A lot of these businesses are bars and night clubs. The owners know the Beat Man by name and you usually build up some kind of a rapport as each wants to scratch the others back a little. The owner wants his place protected even though some of the bars allow the very patrons in that they want protection from. The Police want the cooperation of the businesses in helping to reduce crime and obey the liquor laws. The owner would invite you back to his office and offer you a drink. Its cold out and it would be an insult to refuse the drink, as I am told by Brian. I didn't have to be asked again. I went to private school and never wanted to be rude.

* * *

It's about 9 pm on a Friday night and Brian and I are having a coffee inside a restaurant on the west side of the Granville Mall. There is a male hanging around on the east side walk across the street. The guy is about 32 years old, balding and 5'7" with a slight build. McClay tells me he is a drug trafficker and he carries his stash in his mouth inside a balloon. He goes on to explain they carry the capsule drugs in a balloon in their mouth in case they are jumped by the police. If that happens the drug trafficker will swallow the balloon containing the drugs and extracts it later in the washroom after a bowel movement. Brian has a plan. He tells me he is going to go south on the west side walk and I am to go north on the west sidewalk. We will then both casually cross over to the east side walk and nonchalantly walk towards the balding drug trafficker, McClay from behind and me from in front of the guy. "Ok, then what?" I asked. Brian tells me he will grab the guy from behind and start choking him. I am to punch the guy in the stomach and when it appears he is choking, reach in his mouth and pull out the balloon containing the drugs. It sounds like a plan alright, and all this on my 5th day as a police officer. As instructed I work my way across the street and casually walk towards the drug trafficker as if nothing was wrong. I can see McClay coming up from behind and then grabbing the guy. McClay has a good arm hold around the guy's neck and the guy starts gagging and kicking, called doing the chicken. I know this is my cue and I give the guy a couple of good punches to the mid section. Brian yells" Get the bag, get the bag" and I reach down the guys throat hoping to not lose any fingers, and pull. I proceed to pull out the guys teeth which turn out to be a full dental plate. I yell at Brian "There is nothing there", and show him the guy's dentures. McClay releases his strangle hold and we begin to dust the guy off telling him he is lucky this time. I look around and realize its Friday night and there are buses going by full of Christmas shoppers with their mouths and eyes wide open who have witnessed the entire incident. Welcome to the Granville Mall.

* * *

Brian had an informant who paged him one night when we were working. The informant was at the Yale Hotel beer parlor and he wanted us to come and arrest him because he believed the people he was sitting with thought he was a fink and they were going to do him some harm. McClay and I walk into the bar and do the normal rounds trying to look as natural as possible. When we get to the table with the informant we check everyone's name and then tell the informant there is a warrant for his arrest. The informant puts on a good show and wants to fight. I grab the informant by the shoulders and Brian grabs his legs and we rush to the doors, and with my foot, I kick the fire door handles and it looks like we rammed the guys head into the doors. No sooner are we outside when a young female patron from the bar, about 22 years old, comes up to us screaming that she is a first year law student and she wants to complain about the police violence. I told her to go and graduate and we put the informant in the car and drove off. We all had a good laugh and the informant was thankful we got him out of there. I learned that things are not always as you see them and the law student never knew what really was happening and that we were actually saving this guy from harm.

* * *

I have just started dating a Stewardess named Andrea. After a few weeks she invites me to spend New Years day with her Mother and her Mother's boyfriend at his place in the West End. I meet my girl friend there because she is flying out later that day. I arrive at the apartment at Robson and Denman and wait outside for Andrea to arrive. When she arrives she tells me not to tell Jack, the Mother's boyfriend, what I do for a living because she doesn't think he likes the police. We go inside and I meet Jack who is about 45 years old, his 25 year old son and a bunch of other people who look like Rounders. I tell Jack that I sell insurance. That always gets them off your back, people don't want to be hounded by an insurance salesman much, and everything is cool. As I am sitting in the living room I see a large photo on top of the television. The photo is of Jack and a couple of other guys dressed in fancy fedora hats, dark shirts, white ties and nice suits. It looked like a typical gangster photo without Al Capone. I'm starting to get the idea why Jack may not like what I do. Before I know it I'm into a card game with 3 other guys I just met, nothing serious, I think it was Hearts we were playing. The rest of the day is uneventful but the next day I am at work and go by the robbery office and see a photo of the guy I was just playing cards with at Jack's apartment. The guy is wanted for Armed Robbery. He seemed nice enough when we were playing cards. I advised the Detectives what had happened so they probably got him later.

Having seen the gangster photo of Jack and then his bank robbing friend, I thought I would look into Jack's background a bit. Sure enough after some asking around and looking through files I found Jack's Police record. There were no computers back then that we could quickly retrieve this information from, just plain old digging into files and check cards. Jack was a well known safe cracker and had been a crook for most of his life, having spent some of it behind bars. Well, I thought, I won't be having a lot of family Sunday dinners with this group. I met Jack once more at Andrea's place and the cat was out of the bag. He knew what I did and he knew that I knew what he did. We kept the police to criminal relations conversation to a minimum. Hell, I'm sure he knew more about police work than I did at that point of my career.

The reason I tell this story is it had to have had some effect on my relationship with Andrea because I couldn't be seen with Jack because of my job as I'm sure he couldn't be seen with me because of his associates. He seemed nice enough. Not all crooks are assholes, they are just crooks. Some policemen are assholes but they are on the right side of the law. Had I been in some other profession it may not have mattered what Jack's background was. This would set the tone for my career as it would for any other honest policeman. Be careful picking your friends and watch where you hang out.

The next week I am assigned to a proper field trainer and I take all the boring B&E calls and car accidents. At the conclusion of 3 months I went back to the Police Academy for another 3 months of class room instruction and then graduated as a full 3rd Class Constable. As I am receiving my diploma from the Chief Constable on graduation day he congratulates me and quietly tells me to get a hair cut. My thick hair would curse me for the remainder of my police career. Whenever I would wear a uniform police hat I was always being told to get a hair cut even when I had just got one.

Welcome To Patrol

I am assigned to Team 31, Patrol South working out of the Oakridge sub station. This sub station is a lot more relaxed than Headquarters. There is a parking lot for your private vehicles right at the building and a large grass park right there if you want to go for a run. It was all very convenient. The area I am to patrol is the south side of the city from Ontario Street to Knight Street and 41st Avenue to the Fraser River. There are a lot of Indo Canadians living in the area so some officers call the area Kyber Pass. I will usually have a partner but often I'll be alone. It was nice to have a partner to work with but, of course, it depended who they were.

One of my first days alone I am working day shift and starting to feel pretty comfortable on the job. It's a beautiful day and I'm feeling pretty important in my shiny black and white patrol car. I haven't had any difficult cases yet but could there be anything that I can't handle? I am driving west on 49th Avenue and see a car that I think is speeding. I follow the car as it makes a couple of turns onto different streets and I decide I will have a chat with the driver and put my red light and siren on. I pull the car over in a residential neighborhood and advise the radio operator of the suspect's license plate and my location. Then I walk to the driver's side of the suspect's car and find 3 clean cut males about 19 years old in the vehicle. I ask the driver for his driver's license. He feels the back of his pants as if to be looking for his wallet and says he doesn't have it with him and asks if he can go get it. I ask the driver where he lives and he points to the house we are parked in front of and he says "Right there". I tell him "OK, but get your license and bring it back to my car". I see the 3 young guys casually walk around the side of the house as I return to my police car and I begin to write out a speeding ticket. About 5 minutes go by when an older man taps on the passenger window of my car. He asks "Are you looking for 3 young men?" I say sheepishly "Yeah", beginning to think this is not going to be good. The older man says "They jumped the back fence a couple of minutes ago". Just then the radio operator calls me and advises the car I stopped comes up stolen and she will send a cover unit. What the hell am I going to say? I don't want everyone listening to the radio to know how stupid I was. I tell the operator the cover unit won't be necessary but she could send me a supervisor. I will never make that mistake again, much to the disappointment of some honest people that didn't have their driver's license on them.

* * *

Team 31 was mostly a residential area with a small shopping area on Main Street and Fraser Street with some Commercial businesses, offices and a saw mill at the foot of Fraser Street near the river. Most of the police calls were for Break and Entering, some car accidents and a lot of family disputes. Occasionally, there would be an assistance call to the Blue Boy Hotel because of a bar fight.

One night I am working with Larry Young. Larry and I are about the same age only he has been a policeman for about 6 years and he's a well respected member of the team. We are requested to attend at the Blue Boy Hotel pub regarding a problem patron. When we arrive we are confronted with a male wearing a black Stetson cowboy hat, cowboy boots and the guy is about 6'6" and 250 pounds. According to the bar staff the guy is from out of town and staying at the hotel. The staff advises us the patron had been quite belligerent and trying to start fights. Larry and I know we have to get him out of there but this could be real ugly. We talk really nicely to the guy and explain he has had too much to drink and to keep him safe and out of trouble we want him to go downtown to the jail and sleep it off. We call for the police wagon to transport him to the jail and our cowboy is coming around and is quite agreeable to the action we are taking. The police wagon arrives and it is being driven by a small policewoman from my academy class. We escort cowboy to the back of the wagon and start searching him for any weapons as the policewoman comes around back and says to our prisoner, "OK asshole get in the back of the wagon". Fortunately we had the back door of the wagon open and were able to push the guy inside as he was starting to go crazy. We were pretty pissed off with the policewoman because we had avoided a confrontation all that time and then she has to open her big mouth. I don't know how she made out when she got him down to the jail but we weren't going to find out.

Another night Larry Young and I are dispatched to the Blue Boy Hotel and we arrest 2 guys who had been fighting. They think they are pretty tough and one of the guys looks like he might be. We are trying to talk these guys into the back of the police wagon and they are not complying. When Larry is about to lose his temper he starts calling guys like this, "Sir" and being overly polite. Then Larry would take his eye glasses off and put them in his shirt pocket. When this happens I know the action is about to begin. Larry takes off his glasses and there is a bit of shoving and swearing but we get the two inside the paddy wagon. We follow the wagon to Headquarters so we can assist the lone wagon driver with these guys in taking them to the 5th floor jail

The jail in those days was world renowned for some reason. People used to talk of the elevator ride and what sometimes happened. The elevator back then had a brass railing about waist high that went around the 3 sides of the elevator car. Frank was a civilian elevator operator who sat on a high chair, worked the up and down lever and read a book as he was operating the elevator. I never saw Frank look up from the book, ever. He never wanted to see anything. If there was a complaint, he knew nothing.

The wagon arrives at the rear of the police Headquarters on Main Street and Larry and I prepare to take these two guys up to the jail one at a time. Larry removes his glasses and we call the tougher of the two guys out of the wagon. We walk him over to the elevator door and wait for it to arrive, all the time we are at a fighting stance, waiting for the action to begin. The elevator arrives, the door opens and there is Frank reading his book and the floor and walls inside the elevator are covered in blood. Mr. Tough guy doesn't say a peep as we enter the elevator with Larry staring at him without his glasses on. There was no problem. When we took the second guy from the wagon and up the elevator I thought he was going to be sick. He probably thought the blood was from his buddy. I never did find out where the blood came from but Larry and I laughed because it sure saved us some trouble.

In 1976 the city rolled up the carpet after 2:30 in the morning and went from 4 radio dispatchers to 2. If you worked the midnight shift it was hard to keep your eyes open at times. You would drive around and around your area patrolling and eventually you had to pull over some place to close your eyes. You never really fell asleep because you would jump up if they called you on the radio. It was pretty quiet back then in District 3 anyway.

* * *

I arrived for work one day for afternoon shift and the Sergeant told me I was assigned for the shift at the Headquarters radio room. I drove to Headquarters at 312 Main Street, and introduced myself to the staff in the Communications Section. There would be a Sergeant who was the Chief Dispatch Operator but most of the 5 or 6 staff members were civilians. My job for the evening was to man one of the emergency telephones and then relay the information to the Chief Dispatcher. I was just plunked at the phone without very much instruction and being new as a policeman to boot.

The phone rings and I answer it, "Police, Fire or Ambulance?"
The voice on the phone says "Police, it's Kentucky Fried Chicken
at 70th and Granville and we've just been robbed". I advised the
caller "We will have a car attend immediately," and hung up the
phone. I yelled out that there had been a robbery and the senior
female civilian staff member asked if I still had them on the phone.
I told her no, I had hung up. She went up one side and down the
other giving me supreme shit. Of course I hadn't got a description
of the suspect or a direction of travel other than it was a white
male. I felt pretty stupid but you learned on the fly sometimes.

Once every week or two there would be a stand up parade at the
beginning of the shift where you stood at attention and the Officer
of the day would perform an inspection on everyone as he walked
by the members in their respective lines. The officer was looking
for long hair, improper moustaches, unauthorized equipment such
as speedy loaders, Kel light flashlights and so on. I was always
getting written up for my hair being too long. My hair is thick but
it looked long when I put a hat on and you always had to wear your
hat in those days. This was an era of long hair as the style and you
didn't want to look like a dork when you were off duty so you
pushed the rules. By the time I retired things would have changed
a lot and you would be issued a Kel light flashlight, better guns and
ammunition, body armor and you no longer had to wear a hat, but
not in the 70's.

There was no Police Club at this time and during the summer
months the Beach Patrol officers would confiscate the beer off of
the minors at the beaches, put them on ice and at the end of our
shift we would sit in the St. Johns Ambulance parking lot across
the street from the police station and party. Back then you knew
nobody was going to come and claim their illegal beer. It's
different now. Now you tag the evidence or pour it out because the
parents will come down to the police station and claim the beer and
probably give it back to the kid.

* * *

Larry Young was on holidays and I was assigned to work with this other member Bill Phelps, who was about 4 years senior to me on the job. He meets a girl at one of our after hours parties at the St. Johns Ambulance parking lot and starts taking her out. A couple of nights later we are working the midnight shift and he says we are going to visit her at her apartment in the West Side of Vancouver. This is a long way from Team 31. One thing leads to another and before you know it he is in the bedroom shagging her and I'm sitting in her living room listening to the radio in case we get called. I didn't like that. Not just sitting in the living room and not getting shagged myself, but not even being close or able to respond to a call if we get one.

Bill was pretty infatuated with this girl and he talks me into meeting them again a few nights later around 2 am at the end of our afternoon shift. We meet up and his girl friend has brought along another girl and we are going to go swimming. Bill and I don't have any bathing suits as we weren't expecting to go swimming but the girls unfortunately did. We drive out to the University area, a very posh neighborhood and RCMP territory and my girl says she once lived with her parents at the house we parked in front of. The four of us quietly walk around the side of the house to a large swimming pool located in the back yard about 30 feet from the house which is in darkness. Bill and I take off our clothes and jump into the pool and the girls climb in with their bathing suits on. We're having a good time with lots of giggling. Next thing you know the lights in the back yard go on and this guy comes to the back door and yells "Hey what are you doing?" My girl tells him "Oh, it's ok, I used to live here and we're just having a swim". The guy says ok and closes the door. I thought that's all we need is the guy to call the Mounties as we're skinny dipping in his pool. I could tell my short lived partnership with this guy was just going to be trouble. I was glad to see Larry back at work a couple of weeks later.

* * *

With the boredom came the pranks on midnight shift. Larry and I would be working together and Stan Brown and Dave Bromwell would be working together. There weren't many all night restaurants open back in those days and the manager of the Blue Boy Hotel allowed us to go into their kitchen and make a sandwich for lunch. One night around 3 am Stan and Dave called us and said they wanted to meet us at the Blue Boy Hotel. When Larry and I get there we are hit by water filled balloons from Brown and Bromwell who are on the Hotel roof parking lot about 20 feet above us. This begins a war. A few nights later Stan and Dave want to meet at 48th and Prince Edward, a residential area. Larry and I attend the meet and the other two aren't there yet. We start getting suspicious. I am in the driver's seat and we are parked with the lights off when we see a car coming towards us with its head lights out. I have my window partially open and Larry ducks down so they won't see the reflection of his eye glasses. There is something strange coming out of the approaching cars drivers' window like a trail of smoke. Its Brown and Bromwell and as they get beside us they let go with a fire extinguisher that converts our black and white patrol car to a strictly white car. Now we had to take the car to the car wash before we could turn it in at the station. These two guys are devious, but Larry and I did have a laugh.

The next week Larry and I are requested by Stan and Dave to meet them in front of the Blue Boy Hotel lobby doors. Again it's about 3 in the morning and Larry and I wonder what's coming this time. Stan is driving and Dave is in the passenger seat as they cruise up under the hotel's canopy by the front lobby doors. We know something is up because Dave has a grin on his face a mile wide. As their car approaches Dave's grin changes to a scowl and they quickly drive away. Larry and I wondered what that was all about and tried all night to raise them on the air but they never answered. When we came in to the office at the end of the shift Stan and Dave arrived and told us what happened. They had gone to the Department's maintenance yards and filled a balloon with oil. Dave was holding it in his lap and was going to throw it at us but the oil ate through the balloon as they arrived and covered him and the car. When they drove away they had to take Dave home so he could sit in a bath as the oil was burning his skin and privates. That ended those shenanigans, for a while anyway.

You had to have some fun and laughter because the depressing times would come. You just never knew when that was going to be. Every time the Dispatcher calls your number, 3 alpha 11 or whatever it is, you go OK. What is this one?

I hated going to Sudden Death calls. It was very difficult for me to treat it as just a job when I would be trying to think more about them personally and what got them to this point of death. We are all going to die but can you please die with some dignity.

* * *

It's a Friday in August 1976 and I have been working the day shift alone and will be going home hopefully in an hour. I have entered a Toronto Dominion Bank on Fraser Street to take out some cash for myself. They didn't have ATM machines in those days and banks weren't open on weekends so this is my last chance to get some cash before the bank closes at 3 pm. I am standing in line and one person away from the teller. I have no money on me. I receive a call on my portable radio requesting me to cover another unit at a Sudden Death at a specific address near 39th and Main Street. I reply "10-4" even though it's not my patrol area, and I continue to wait in line at the bank. I get my money from the teller and start to return to my car when the operator calls me again. I advise her I'm on my way and wonder what the hurry is. I have been to a couple of sudden deaths before involving elderly people and the dead person isn't going any where, their dead. I am driving north on Fraser Street approaching 41st Avenue with about a mile to go and the operator tells me to go code 3, emergency lights and siren. I arrive at the location and it is a low income, three storey apartment complex and there are several fire trucks sitting outside the building. The police car that works the area and is assigned this call isn't there yet. As I'm gathering things I think I will need, there is a fireman at the door of the complex frantically waving for me to come. I walk inside the suite and the firemen are with a young fellow, about 16 years old who is sitting on the couch and one of the fire fighters says "She is in there", pointing towards the bathroom. I walk into the bathroom and there is a young 10 year old girl fully clothed lying on her back in the bath tub and she is soaking wet. Her eyes are partially open and she has bubbles coming from her nose and mouth. I tell the fireman "She is still breathing" and he says "No, she is dead, it's just air escaping from her lungs." Finally the police officer who was assigned to the case, Pat McFee, a more experienced officer than me, arrives at the scene and to take over because I am in shock. The fireman tells me the 16 year old boy stabbed the girl and I end up hand cuffing the kid and placing him under arrest. One of my own children was the same age as the victim and you think to yourself that you would like to beat the creep to a pulp, but you don't. You have been trained to try and deal with it in a professional and matter of fact way so not to jeopardize the case.

I thought McFee knew what he was doing but he didn't. He made some phone calls from the crime scene calling the arrested boy's and victim's mothers about the incident. That should never have been done. He should never have used the phone at the crime scene and the victim's mother should have been spoken to in person.

By the time we left the apartment with the 16 year old suspect there was a huge crowd out front including the media with their cameras. Pat McFee went to the City Morgue that was right next door to the downtown police station and I went to the Homicide office and sat in on the interview with the Detective and the accused. The accused was wearing a prison jump suit made of paper at this time and was very calm and matter of fact. There was no emotion from him at all.

It turns out the 16 year old stabbed the girl on a dare as he thought he could get away with murder. He had this elaborate scheme of disposing of the body in a dumpster so as to not get caught. The young suspect had thought this whole thing out and he said in the interview that without a body the police had no case. He had a different victim in mind at first, a 3 year old child that lived across the street, but they weren't home so he invited this young girl over to play hide and seek at his apartment. She hid in the bath tub and he stabbed her 47 times before turning on the shower to wash all the blood away. He was found guilty and spent three years at the Willingdon Youth Detention Center. After he served those three years he was given a new identity. I have never gotten over that case and shed some tears at times.

* * *

I am working alone and get a call to a sudden death on the top floor of this old house. The ambulance attendants are there and the family is down stairs on the main floor. I go up stairs and this little old lady has died and is still sitting in her rocking chair. When someone is definitely dead the Ambulance attendants don't always remove the body. In this case they wanted me to call the Coroner and have them attend. I make the call and the Coroner arrives in a white Budget Rent a Truck with a cheap home made sign on the side of the truck saying 'Coroner'. I am told that the regular Coroner's vehicle is in the body shop for repairs. The Coroner's assistant comes up the stairs which are very narrow and asks me if I can take the ladies jewelry off her finger. Rigor mortis has set in and the lady is stiff as a board. I tell the guy I can't do it. He was very nice and said he will do it. He then proceeds to bend the fingers to a terrible cracking noise and removes the ring. He then lifts the old gal out of the chair and lays her on her back on the floor but she is still in a sitting position. He bends her out of that position with the same cracking noise and places her in a body bag and onto a dolly. The assistant then proceeds to bounce the dolly with the covered body securely attached to the dolly down the stairs and out to the rented Coroners van. I thought where is the dignity?

A few weeks after this incident Larry and I covered Howard Dixon, a new recruit on our team, at a sudden death. I think it was Howard's first sudden death and he was a little apprehensive of what to do. When we arrived we looked in the bedroom and saw an older deceased male lying in bed and at the foot of the bed were 2 artificial legs. I told Howard he could advise the Coroner he wouldn't need the rented van but an Austin Mini will do.

I arrive for work on afternoon shift and Brian McGee a fellow constable only from District Four has asked Larry and me if we would cover him as he executes a search warrant in the Marpole area. Brian was an English fellow and had previously been a Bobby in England before joining the Vancouver Police Department. Brian was a hold-over of the anti drug era from the late 60's and early 70's and had a reputation for being overly zealous towards the drug activity where a lot of the members were beginning to let things go. Apparently on his way to work Brian had spotted a Marijuana plant growing on the balcony of an apartment building and he had gone downtown to the Justice of the Peace office and obtained a search warrant. Larry and I follow Brian to the apartment building and we gain entry into the building and go up to the suite in question. Larry and I stand back as Brian knocks on the door of the suite. The tenant comes to the door and asks what the problem is. Brian tells the tenant he has a search warrant for the suite because of the plant that is on his balcony. The tenant responds with "You mean the bamboo plant?" Larry and I started to slowly walk away very embarrassed and yet thinking this was pretty funny. We never covered Brian again.

* * *

One day Larry Young and I get called to a sudden death at a Seniors Home near 52nd and Prince Albert Street. The unit is set for independent living and they are well cared for duplex cottages. The ambulance was on the scene when we arrive. The victim was an elderly lady and she was lying on the bathroom floor with her head stuck to the top ledge of the bath tub. It was obvious rigor mortis had set in. She had a large blanket that went down to her feet and was completely wrapped around her. The smell in the suite was unbearable, particularly when she was moved and her body fluids released. It looked as if she had fallen and hit her head on the side of the tub. It was early spring but the place was about 100 degrees inside. In the living room was a wall mounted heater that only had an on off switch and no thermostat. The switch was on and the walls were very hot to touch. They were so hot that we called the Fire Department to attend. It appeared that the lady was cold during the night and turned on the heat to warm up. Sometime later, with the blanket around her, she went to the bathroom and probably tripped on the blanket striking her head on the ledge of the bath tub. I have seen my own family members on a cold day walking around with a blanket wrapped around them and I would lecture them and tell them this story and how dangerous it is.

* * *

The liquor laws in the City of Vancouver as well as the Province of British Columbia were pretty archaic in the early 1970's. Liquor stores and bars were not allowed to be open on Sundays and to get a drink with alcohol in a restaurant you had to order food. There were some places that would put an old dried up cheese sandwich on your table in case the police or a liquor inspector walked in and the server would take the sandwich back when you left. There may have been one neighborhood pub given a license back then with many applications appearing before the Liquor Control Board.

An Englishman opened a little restaurant at 49th and Main and he was trying to use it as a neighborhood pub. It really was a hole in the wall and our Sergeant wanted Larry and I to go in and get a drink because the Sergeant didn't think this guy was following the rules. We enter the restaurant wearing tennis shorts and shirts and ask the owner for a menu. The owner replied with a curt "No food, only beer." Larry and I sat down and had two beers and then returned to the office to complete our reports. The guy was shut down the next day by the Liquor Control Board.

* * *

I am working alone one night as Larry has taken the night off. The dispatcher comes on the air and advises all units that there is a man with a knife at Ontario and South West Marine Drive. I arrive just as my old horseplay buddies, Bromwell and Brown are arriving. There is an older male about 50 years old on the front lawn of a house and he is holding a large butcher knife and he is obviously distraught. We approach him and he starts yelling at us and we draw our guns to have at the ready. We keep our distance but circle around him. He would concentrate on one of us and then run toward us swinging the knife. I would run away and the other two officers would get closer from behind, pleading for him to drop the knife. The guy would then turn on the other two and run at them while I would move in closer from behind. It was like a Mexican standoff. We didn't want to shoot him, and as long as we could stay a safe distance and he didn't go back in the house there didn't seem a need to. The shift supervisor, Corporal Ian Young, arrived at the scene and saw his three men running around the front lawn, back and forth with their guns drawn and this old guy brandishing a butcher knife. The suspect eventually ran out of steam and dropped the knife and we took him into custody and eventually to the Psych Ward at the hospital. The three of us received a Commendation for not shooting the guy.

* * *

I am working alone one night and I get a call about a female down on Knight Street. I attend at the location and the woman about 30 years old is right out of it either on drugs or drunk. I arrest her and call for the paddy wagon to attend. When the wagon arrives I assist the wagon driver putting the female into the back of the police wagon. The woman lays a big greenie right into my face. Without a thought my instant response was a good smack across the side of her head with my open hand. I find there is nothing more degrading than to have someone spit on you. I would rather be soundly punched by someone than to be spit on. I never received a complaint.

* * *

Larry and I are working the 8pm to 4 am shift and we are a plain clothes unit. We get a call around 2 am to attend a suspicious circumstances call in the 800 block of East 6th Avenue. This is not our patrol area but there are no other cars available. The apartment building is notorious for drug types and lowlifes. We arrive and ring the buzzer. A male answers the intercom and we tell him it's the police. The guy for some reason doesn't believe us and won't open the front door. The guy eventually arrives at the front door and after showing our badges we convince him who we are and he lets us in. The guy is acting a little strange and while we are walking down the hall towards his suite he says he called the police because his girl friend is sick. We walk inside the suite and he leads us to the bedroom door. Inside the bedroom is a female about 25 years old lying on her back on top of the bed, wearing only a pair of blue jeans. Her head is to the side, eyes partially open and her tank top has been ripped off exposing her breasts and she has no shoes on. There is a sofa in the room beside the bed and there is a large butcher knife resting on top of it. There is a large amount of green matter on the floor beside the bed where the victims head is. Larry checks for a pulse and determines the female is dead and he says so. We escort the male out of the bedroom, close the bedroom door and call for an ambulance even though we think she is dead. The male rushes the bedroom door because he wants to go back inside but we won't let him and the fight is on. We hand cuff him and arrest him until we can figure out what has happened here. Things look suspicious in the bedroom and we don't know if we have a homicide or a drug overdose. Now we have the ambulance and the police wagon coming. I went back inside the bedroom and took another look at the victim. She has a small amount of blood exiting the corner of her mouth which wasn't there when we first arrived. I thought to myself maybe Larry's death assessment was wrong. The ambulance arrives and they confirm she is dead and they leave leaving the victim in the bedroom. The victim has to stay there until Major Crime arrives as this may be a homicide scene. Major crime arrives and then the Coroner who takes the female away in the usual black body bag. I called the Coroner in the morning after we finished our reports because I was so bothered about the blood from the victim's mouth and wondered if she could have been alive when Doctor Larry made his professional assessment. The Coroner determined the death was a drug overdose and it was not unusual that the blood could work its way up to the mouth after some time as a result of the violent wrenching of the green matter that was on the floor.

* * *

I am working one night around 11 pm with Barry McKew and we are parked at the corner of Kingsway and Rupert. Barry has been driving but he is talking to a girl friend on the pay phone at the north east corner. The emergency alarm goes off on the car radio and the dispatcher advises that there is a robbery in progress at a pizza restaurant at Kingsway and McHardy one block from our location. I start honking the horn to tell Barry to get off the phone and I see another patrol car go by us code 3 with Alex MacDonald and Bob Malloy. Alex and Bob go to the front of the restaurant and Barry and I go to the back where I get out of the car. I can see somebody at the top of the outside stairs at the rear of the restaurant lying down. Alex MacDonald exits the back door near the body and yells there was a witness chasing the suspect and the guy at the top of the stairs has been stabbed. A dog man arrives and he and the dog start following the scent at the rear of the building and I accompany him with my gun out as a cover man for him. It is pitch black out and the dog is hot on the trail and he's leading us through some back yards with heavy brush. I am pretty scared and have my finger on the trigger for one of the few times in my whole career. The dog leads us around the yard sniffing and then out to the west side walk of McHardy Street where we find the witness lying on the sidewalk stabbed to death. All hell has broken loose. We have a guy stabbed at the top of the stairs who is now on route to the hospital and a witness dead on the sidewalk. Everyone is searching the area for the suspect but with no luck. The mother and brother of the owner of the pizza place are at the restaurant and the Sergeant in charge tells McKew and I to take them code 3 to the hospital as the brother's condition is grave. We arrive at the Vancouver General Emergency Ward and the Doctors are working on the Restaurant owner. We can see them using the defibulator on his heart and they ask us to wait in the waiting room. I sit with the mother and brother while Barry seems to be hustling up some good looking nurse. The Doctor comes into the waiting room and advises the family they couldn't save the victim and he has passed away. The brother goes crazy and I'm wrestling with him in the waiting room as he wants to go back inside the Emergency Ward where his dead brother is. The family is of Greek heritage and the mother is screaming and yelling and I am trying to calm them both down while Barry continues with his smooth moves on the nurse. I wasn't happy with Barry as I'm confronted with these hysterical people and he's too busy trying to hustle some woman. We had two dead people for a robbery that turned out to be a $100 take. I never did find out who was responsible for the murders. I enquired at the Homicide Section a few years later when I had an occasion to be in their office and I was told they had a drug addict responsible but he later died of an overdose before being arrested. As a Constable you attend the calls and do as much as you can but you turn things over to the Detectives when they arrive and then you get back to your regular duties, sometimes not learning of the outcome.

* * *

I am working another night with Barry McKew when there is a man with a knife call in the area of East 22nd and Beatrice. The Sergeant, George Charuk wants to meet all the attending units a block away. We meet and George says he wants 2 guys at each corner of the house and he says, "What the hell, the rest of us will take the bull by the horns and go up the front steps". As we are walking toward the house George has a fellow with him in plain clothes. George introduces us to his friend Goldie who is riding along with him and he tells us Goldie is a retired Vancouver Policeman that had to retire because he was losing his eye sight. The four of us walk up the front steps of this old house and an Indo Canadian male comes to the front door. George tells the guy why we are there and suggests to his buddy Goldie that he search the guy for old time sake. Goldie has the suspect facing him and he pats him down and tells George he's clean, no weapons. George then walks up the stairs inside the house to the living room followed by Goldie and then followed by the suspect. Right behind the suspect is Barry and then me. Barry yells out "What the hell is this"? There is a wooden handle sticking out of the guys blue jeans at the back of his pants. Barry pulls on the handle and removes a meat cleaver that the guy had stuffed down the pants. I guess Goldie was blinder than George thought.

* * *

I always hated attending car accidents. While it wasn't pleasant, I could handle dealing with dead people but I dreaded dealing with injured people that were looking to me for medical assistance or comfort. I wasn't good at it. When I was in the academy we had a middle aged British woman as our first aid instructor. She was a delightful woman with a great sense of humor. She would show up at class with several of these dummy's from the waist up that you would practice CPR and mouth to mouth on. In her high pitched English voice she would yell out "The patient has stopped breathing" and we would do our Doctor Kildare routine on the dummy and give mouth to mouth and CPR and bring it back to life. It was more fun when we would practice on a real person like one of the female classmates. The instructor showed up at class one day with a skeleton in order to discuss the anatomy and a student named Ed passed out and fell to the floor at his desk. He was turfed out from the Academy that day.

* * *

One sunny Sunday afternoon I am working alone in my marked police car and the radio operator requests that I attend a Motor Vehicle accident at South East Marine Drive and Knight Street and an ambulance is on the way. I arrive at the scene and there is a small car that had taken the off ramp from the Knight Street Bridge and the car is resting against a light standard. It doesn't look like there is any damage at all to the car. Inside the car behind the wheel is good looking Italian male about 25 years old and he is slumped over to the side unconscious. Remembering my First Aid class, I tilt the guys head back, check the air wave and then begin to give him mouth to mouth resuscitation. I can hear the siren from the ambulance as it is getting nearer and there is a crowd gathering around the car to see if I can bring this guy back to life. Thank God the ambulance attendants arrive and take over. The guy is still unconscious and they remove him very carefully from the car and place him on one of those wooden boards for back injuries. The ambulance takes him away with their emergency equipment on and I feel good that I kept this guy alive until they got there. I have the vehicle towed away and return to the Oakridge Police Sub Station to finish my reports. I phone the

General Hospital to see how the victim is doing and they tell me they released him a while ago. I am amazed as I thought he was near death. I complete my accident report and drive to the victim's house as I am curious about his instant recovery. I ask the fellow how he is feeling and I make a joke about how our lips were locked as I was giving him mouth to mouth resuscitation. He doesn't crack a smile. I thought screw you buddy; you wasted my whole afternoon on this case. It turned out he was getting married the next week and he had a panic attack as he was exiting the bridge.

* * *

Late one night I am dispatched to a major car accident at 33rd and Knight Street. The Dispatcher advises me that people are trapped in a car and the Fire Department is on the way. I am working alone and speed to the scene code 3. I arrive and I am the first car there. There is a large crowd of people standing around the west side of the street and sure enough there is a car upside down lying on its roof near the curb. There are 4 people still inside the car and none of the bystanders are rendering any assistance but just looking. I am bending over to look inside the car when wham, someone punched me in the right side of my head knocking off my hat. I looked around and saw some guy at the front of the crowd who looked like he wanted me to respond to the punch and he wanted to fight me. I thought this isn't the time to save your dignity. I have trapped people in the over turned vehicle. The ambulance and cover cars arrived pretty fast but I never saw the fighter again. One for the bad guys but I will have my day.

Other than my room mate, I am seeing less and less of my old rugby friends. The shift work didn't help or the different days off. It's difficult to get a group together to go partying on a Tuesday night. I see them at rugby practice and game days but I think my profession is a threat to them. They don't trust me I guess, thinking because I'm a cop that I will go after them for any little infraction. Keeping in mind it's the mid 70's and I'm about 30 years old and there is a lot of dope being passed around between my rugby friends and I have to stay clear of it as much as I can. On the other hand, like so many police officers, you get wrapped up in your work and the only people who understand what you're talking about are other police officers. This has been referred to as the Thin Blue Line.

* * *

The cars in those days didn't have automatic door locks like they do now. In fact they didn't have the release where the driver could unlock the passenger's door; you had to lean over the front seat to do it.

I'm on duty alone in a marked patrol car and I have parked in the White Spot Restaurant parking lot at Marine and Ross Street and had car service. When I finish lunch I leave the car and go inside to the restroom. On my return I discover I have locked my keys inside the car. There I am, in uniform, with a coat hanger trying to break into my own car. I got the door open but I'm sure all the other patrons had a good laugh at the sight of this dumb cop locked out of his own car.

Another occasion Dave Dawson and I had been called to a sudden death at an old folk's home and when we returned to the car I unlocked my door and threw the car keys over the roof of the car for Dave to unlock his side. He missed the keys and they fell into a storm sewer. We have to go back into the old folk's home, get a coat hanger and try and retrieve the keys. There we are on our hands and knees in uniform, trying to hook the keys from the sewer. It took a while but we did it.

* * *

In the mid to late 70's there was only one place to hold the drunks that you found on the street and that was the Police Drunk Tank. It was basically a large tiled room that had several drains on the floor so that the room could be washed out every morning from the drunks urinating all over the floor and each other. There was no civilized Detox unit that there is now and often the Drunk Tank was full. It wasn't uncommon at this particular time if the Drunk

Tank was full to take an annoying drunk for a ride to the City limits, dump him out of the Police wagon and let him sober up by walking back

Dave Dawson and I are working together and we pick up a drunken 17 year old Native kid about 2 am and take him home to his parents near 63rd and Knight Street. Dave walks up to the front door and I stay in the car with the kid. Our vehicle is the cage type 4 door car with the glass partition between the front and back seat where the kid is. The kid starts acting up and swearing at me and kicking the glass partition. Then the kid starts spitting on the glass with this disgusting saliva running down the partition. Dave returns to the car as the parents are either not home or won't answer the door. When Dave sees what the kid has been doing he drives away from the house and we go south on Knight Street and into Richmond. We drive west on Westminster Highway and then north on Highway 99 and we pull over. We open the back door and throw the kid out of the car and he falls into a big drainage ditch and we drive away. You would never do that now but that's what you did 35 years ago.

* * *

I am the low man on the seniority list so when ever another squad needs a body they call up the less senior person. I am requested to attend at the Marine Squad for two days to fill in. Because Vancouver has a large waterfront as well as Marinas and beaches, the city has the responsibility for policing the Vancouver waters as well as the city proper. My room mate was a fisherman and I liked boats so I figure this might be a nice job as the weather has been beautiful the past week. I arrive at the police boat house at the north foot of Columbia Street where it meets Burrard Inlet and there are about 3 real senior guys there. I am told to put my lunch away and sit down and deal. We play cards for 6 hours when I finally ask "When do we take the boat out?" One of the guys relents and says "Ok, we'll take the boat for a spin". The next day was the same. Welcome to the Marine Squad kid. That was it for me. I never set foot on the boat again.

* * *

I am attending Provincial Court at 222 Main Street on a minor theft from auto case. I am waiting in the hall outside the court room for the case to start when the lawyer for the accused approaches me and we make small talk. I get called into the court room, get sworn in and give my evidence in chief. The same lawyer begins to cross exam me and asks if I can pick out his client from the viewers in the court room? I had heard of this being done before but I thought the old stories were a joke. This lawyer was serious. I said "yes Your Honor, that is the accused sitting to the left of his brother in the second row". The lawyer went pale and asked how I could be so sure, as the brothers are twins but not identical. I told the court that Larry Young and I would play touch football with the neighborhood kids when we were walking the Fraser Street beat and we played with the brother of the accused. I guess that was the defense because there were no further questions.

* * *

The police rugby team convinced me to play with their squad and we had a game against UBC one Saturday. During the game I was accidentally kicked in the head by an opponent and I required stitches and wound up with a great shiner around my left eye. I had to work the next two weeks looking like I got the worse for wear in a fight and I received a lot of strange looks and comments from the public.

On a beautiful sunny Saturday in September 1977 I am in the best physical shape of my life and I'm at a Kats rugby practice as the beginning of the season is only weeks away. We have formed a loose scrum and I get hit on my right side by one player and then simultaneously on the left side by a different player. The MCL of my left knee snaps and I am writhing in pain on the ground until the knee has gone numb. They dragged me off the field and someone took my jersey and left me on the sidelines. I got a friend to drive me to St. Paul's Emergency and I am operated on the next morning. When I wake up I'm in a cast up to my left hip and I'm going to be off work for some time. I only have enough sick time built up at work for 2 weeks off. I am then assigned to light duties at the Fraser Street Police Office. The office is on the second floor of a walk up building and I have to wear a shirt and tie and I have my gun on my hip and crutches. I read a lot of books because being on the second floor not many people knew we had an office there. I was just as glad.

After several months I have recovered from my knee surgery and I am back on the road. I am getting tired of Patrol and would like to get into my dream job of being a motorcycle cop. I would go downtown to the Traffic Division and see Staff Sergeant McLarty who was second in charge. He would try and discourage me about applying because I am now 31 years old and he believes one's bones don't heal very well after an accident at that age. I would leave his office discouraged as this is what I really wanted to do.

In September 1978 I get married for the second time. It's a small wedding with mostly family members but I have my old partner and friend Larry Young and his wife Stella attend the wedding.

I decide to apply for the Emergency Response Team. This is equivalent to the American SWAT Team. We have all the physical and emotional tests and when they get to the short list they turn me down because I am recently married and they don't think this would be a good thing for me at least for a couple of years. They do encourage me to apply for the Containment Team of the same unit. It's not the same. You don't rappel down the side of buildings and other dangerous things but I apply and get accepted into the Containment Unit while Larry was accepted into the regular ERT.

* * *

I am sent on loan to District 1 for a few weeks as they are low on man power. I thought that's ok, I haven't worked there since I first started the job and the change of scenery would be good. It's about 2:30 am and I am working the midnight shift with one of my Academy classmates, Vicki Matheson in the West End area. I am driving the marked police car east on Georgia Street and we stop at a red light at Burrard. I look to my left and I see two males in the middle of the 600 block of Burrard Street fighting using their fists and feet. I make a left turn and start in their direction, north on Burrard and the two fighting males move towards the east side curb and continue fighting. As I pull the car up beside them, one of the males walks away from the area of the curb but the other male is still lying there. Vicki and I get out of the car with our 24 inch wooden batons that were issued at that time and discover that everything seems under control. The fight has stopped and there doesn't seem to be any threat to us, but the guy in the curb has not moved. We call for an Emergency Ambulance and a Supervisor. The ambulance takes the male victim away to St.Paul's Hospital and Vicki and I continue getting people's names and addresses and their description of what had transpired here. The Supervisor calls us on the radio and advises the male was DOA, Dead On Arrival, and to bring in the 3 people to Headquarters for questioning.

We are wondering how this could happen as it didn't look like a particularly vicious fight with weapons. It turned out from the autopsy that the male had died from a brain aneurism   The Doctor said he wasn't surprised as the males knuckles were all scarred from street fighting. The Doctor said sometimes a sign of an aneurism is a bad temper resulting from pressure on the brain. That made sense to me anyway. I had an uncle that died at a young age from a brain aneurism. He was a pretty good hockey player in the 1940's but he was a big fighter with a bad temper. The Major Crime Squad charged the surviving male with Manslaughter but the case was eventually thrown out of court.

* * *

During my time working Patrol I had 2 car accidents with my patrol car. Both times I had my emergency lights and siren on and my car was struck as I was slowly going through a red light at an intersection on the way to a call. It was just by chance I am sure, that both drivers were members of a minority group but not the same group. There were no injuries and the damage in both accidents was minimal because we were all fortunately going very slowly through the intersection. They were driving through a green light and me through a red light. When an officer gets involved in an accident or causes damage to the City's police car there are lots of reports and a Police Supervisor has to attend the scene. Then the Accident Review Board looks at the accident and determines the officer's culpability in the incident. If you are found at fault this could affect your own private car insurance rates so you sweat for several months awaiting the outcome. In my accidents they found it was a risk of the job and no action was taken against me.

* * *

Everyone is required to do their inside time. Inside time is either working in the Jail, the radio room or the Public Information Counter. My Sergeant approached me and asked if I would work the Fraser Street Police Office and this would count as my inside time. As I was newly married and the job was weekends off, I thought I would take the job for six months. This was a different office than the one I worked in after my rugby accident. This office was on the ground floor with a desk and chair at the front of the building and then a wall and door that led to a very large back room for meetings. The previous tenant had been a child care facility which seemed appropriate that we would follow. The Team 31 members were encouraged to come by and complete their police reports at the office using the meeting room facilities in the back instead of sitting inside a restaurant to complete the reports.

One day my old pals Bromwell and Brown arrive to do their reports and maybe just harass me for fun. At the very back of the meeting room was an old kitchen and it contained some small jars of paint that might have been used at some time for finger painting left over from the previous tenant, the Day Care. Its Halloween time and the fire crackers are out. Stan and Dave are throwing a few fire crackers around my office when one of them gets an idea. Dave takes the lid off a jar of blue paint and puts a fire cracker inside the jar and lights the fuse. It worked very well. There was paint over all four walls in the kitchen area and we laughed our heads off. Then Bromwell and Brown decided it was time to get out of there and I was stuck with the mess and clean up.

The latter part of August I go away to England for 3 weeks to play rugby and when I return I once again go to the Traffic Office and I finally convince S/Sgt McLarty to accept me into the Traffic Division and fulfill my dream as a motorcycle cop. Within 2 weeks I am transferred to Traffic and out of the Fraser Street Police office.

Work Hard, Play Hard

It's October 1979 and I attend at the Police Stores and pick up my new Motorcycle uniform which consisted of hand me down motorcycle boots, helmet and breeches, those puffy pants that make you look like you have swollen hips. Then I am given a bunch of ticket books and I realize that I'm not crazy about writing tickets but I sure like that shiny, throaty Harley Davidson motorcycle. I will adjust.

There are eight new traffic members and we are all told to meet at the Pacific National Exhibition parking lot in the east end of the city to commence training. The motorcycle is a Harley Davidson 1300cc Road King Police Special and it weighs about 800 pounds. Fortunately the bikes we are learning on are not new and we learn how to pick them up after we have accidently dropped them. I sat on the bike and started it up. It sounded great, just like I dreamed of but I was surprised at the amount of vibration from the engine. We started off slowly, learning to release and ride the clutch and change gears. Even though we were being trained by the Department's designated Motorcycle Training Instructor, Gerry Hanson, we would have to pass a driving test at the Provincial Motor Vehicle Testing Station. Part of the road test requires that you maneuver the bike through red cones or pilings. This is the same test that all new motorcyclists are required to take regardless of the bike; they could be on a small 250cc motorcycle. We have to be able to get our 1300cc Harley Davidson complete with large saddle bags and crash bar through the same designated cones as the small bikes. It didn't seem fair but it would make us better riders for it.

After the first day of training I went home and could hardly bend my wrist because of the constant hand clutch action. The day was continuous in and out of the pilings, ride the clutch, ride the back brake and keep the shiny side up. Just when you got confident and thought you could ride, Gerry Hanson would move the pilings closer together, nearer to the testing dimensions that we will have to pass. This would be repeated a few more times until we were at the testing dimensions and almost ready for the road test. We now had the use of our own assigned motorcycle and Gerry would lead us around the City of Vancouver checking out different areas and getting more comfortable with our new equipment. We looked like a bunch of Ducklings, single file following behind Mother Goose, Gerry Hanson.

It was the fall season and Vancouver gets a lot of rain and fallen leaves on the roadway. We would be working and writing tickets in bad weather and had to learn to ride using a leather lap robe. If it rained the lap robe was attached to the crash bars of the motorcycle and you placed it over the lower part of your body in order to keep part of you dry. Heaven for bid, you don't want to get hemorrhoids, often caused from the cold and wet seat. We had to experience driving over the wet leaves lying on the road and even the white traffic lines when they are wet. On a rainy day when you changed lanes you could feel the bike skid over the white lines. It scared the shit out of me at first but you got used to it. I don't think the City had the best quality tires on the bikes in those days.

* * *

We had been in training for about 3 weeks and for some reason there were just three of us at this one days training session, Gerry Hanson, Alex MacDonald and myself. It was a partly cloudy but dry day and Gerry thought this would be a good day for something different. We are dressed in plain clothes and started riding east out the Lougheed Highway. I realize as we are following Gerry, we're just two ducklings instead of the usual eight. We had been riding for sometime and before I knew it we were out near Mission B.C., maybe 50 miles from Headquarters. We were getting hungry and stopped at a place called the Sasquatch Inn. We ordered a hamburger and decided to have a couple of beers to go with it. After lunch we started our ride home. It was getting late but it was still light out and we needed to get the bikes back to the police garage. We were driving through a large farm area where there were not many houses, still riding single file and going about 100 km/h. As we are coming near a farm house a large German shepherd dog catches my eye as the dog stands up as Gerry drives by the house. The dog starts barking and running towards the road and I can see him approaching Alex who is about 100 yards behind Gerry. The dog runs onto the road and stands in front of Alex's bike. Alex had no chance. He hit the dog killing it and Alex laid the bike down on its side and riding, or should I say sliding, with the bike still under him, to a large 6 foot drainage ditch beside the road. The bike went into the ditch but Alex stopped short of it. He was ok but shaken. I was too. I saw the whole thing unfold and wondered how I would have handled it. We had to call the Abbotsford Police and get a tow truck. We talked to the dog's owner and completed an accident report at the side of the road. Alex got a ride back to Vancouver with the tow truck and Gerry and I started to ride back. It began to rain and Gerry got us onto the #1 Highway as it would be faster. I was scared to death. I am sure Gerry felt fine but I was doing 100 km/h as the cars were passing me throwing up rain in my face as they sped by. My lap robe was flapping around and the motorcycle shaking like crazy and I hoped I wouldn't touch one of those dreaded white traffic lines. Let's say I didn't think I looked cool at that particular time.

* * *

The big day arrives to take the road test at the testing station. We all go out to the station in Burnaby and take our turn. I ride through the cones laid out in their parking lot and I don't knock any over and then the instructor tells me to exit the lot and go north on Wayburne Drive and then come back. I get to the exit and I see a car coming from the south and decide I have time to turn left and go north before the car gets too close. I exit the parking lot, lean the bike to the left and proceed to go north on Wayburne. Unfortunately I was in such a rush to get going I didn't realize there was a median in the middle of the road and I couldn't get over to the right hand side and had to continue north on the wrong side of the road. I failed the test and had to come back the next day.

The next day I arrived at the testing station with Bob Malloy who is filling in for Gerry Hanson who is away on vacation. I enter the building dressed in full motorcycle police uniform and announce I am here to take the test. The lady behind the counter says, "Oh, you're Wrong Way Barker." I was already famous at the Motor Vehicle Branch. I sheepishly admit I am and then I proceed to pass the test with no problem. I can't wait to get out of there and hope I never see these people again. Talk about being embarrassed. Malloy and I go for coffee and it starts to rain slightly. We leave the coffee shop and start riding west on 41st Avenue in Vancouver. I am riding my Harley Davidson and Malloy is riding a Kawasaki motorcycle that the Department is testing out. We are riding side by side down a slight hill approaching Rupert Street where there is a large semi trailer truck partly in the intersection waiting to complete a left turn to go north on Rupert Street. The light at Rupert changes to yellow and Malloy and I start to brake to come to a stop for the upcoming red light. Malloy stops and I have only applied my back brake and I'm not stopping. The light changes to red and the semi trailer unit starts to make his left turn and I am still sliding with my back wheel locked. Everything was happening in slow motion as my ass was going from side to side trying to keep the bike upright and I could see the truck driver's eyes in shock. I saw the front left portion of the truck at my left side and I gave my hips a quick move to the right and the bike cleared the front of the truck. The truck made its left turn and I pulled over to the side of the road and stopped. Bob Malloy pulled up beside me and told me to turn the bike off. I already had but I was shaking so much it just looked like the bike was running. Here I am, I just got my license and almost died within the hour. Is this what I really wanted to do?

It's a great feeling riding a motorcycle but you have to ride defensively. There is no protection and even if you're wearing a helmet and you get airborne you're probably toast. As a motorcycle cop your chances of an accident are even greater because of the amount of traffic on the road and you are out there for 8 to 10 hours a day and riding in all kinds of weather. The risk further increases when you end up taking chances as you go after someone to give them a ticket. In the Traffic Division there was always somebody off injured.

Now that the eight new Ducklings have passed the road test we are sent to our respective Squads and told to go out and write traffic tickets. Chris Bayne, another new guy in Traffic and I are watching a stop sign at Arbutus and 8th Avenue one afternoon shift. A car runs the stop sign and Chris goes after him on his motorcycle and I wait for the next potential violator. About 15 minutes has gone by and no one else has run the stop sign but Chris hasn't returned to our spot yet and I wonder what happened to him. I leave my position and go south on Arbutus and find Chris laying in the middle of the intersection of Arbutus and Broadway with the ambulance sirens in the background and on their way to Chris's aid. Chris broke his wrist and I think that just about finished Chris off as a motorcycle cop.

In the Traffic Division you are expected to write at least 200 tickets per month, it sounds like a lot but it really isn't. That's only 10 tickets a day which gives you room for some quality tickets like red lights and stop signs and if you are shy on the number there is always the public's favorite, radar. In the 1970's and 80's most moving violation tickets such as speeding were not fines like today but a point system. A speeding ticket was 3 points on your driver's license and the Motor Vehicle Department allowed a maximum of 3 points per year without any further penalty. If there were no further tickets that year your 3 points were erased from your license. More than 3 points and you may receive an additional fine or perhaps lose your drivers license. Because of the point system some drivers weren't as irate as others when they received a ticket because it didn't cost them anything so I didn't feel bad handing out 200 tickets a month.

* * *

My third shift in traffic and I'm on afternoons, 4pm to midnight. There is another Doug on the squad so I am given the nick name Spike for some unknown reason. I am getting ready to leave the office and make the one block walk to the police garage where the motorcycles are kept. The Corporal, Bob Delf is a dead ringer, cigar and all, for Jackie Gleeson, the actor/comedian. Bob has been a policeman at this point about 30 years and has been in traffic forever. As I'm leaving the office he tells me they are all meeting for dinner at the Yen Lok Restaurant on East Pender Street at 6pm and I should be there. I cruise around on my motorcycle for a couple of hours, give out a few tickets and drive to the Yen Lok. I park out front and I don't see another bike in sight. I didn't know at the time that they park in the back alley so as to not draw any attention to themselves. It's about 6:15 pm and everyone should be here. I walk inside the front door and an Asian male tells me the other officers are at the back of the restaurant behind a bamboo screen. Sure enough there they are, maybe 10 guys sitting around starting to fill their faces. The Asian waiter asks me if I want some cold tea. He points to somebody pouring their cold tea and it looks very much like beer in a Chinese teapot. I realize I have died and gone to Heaven. The cold tea flows and the food is the finest Chinese food around. The Sergeant, Dave Zurr and Bob Delf are having a scotch as we peons have cold tea. After finishing the meal the waiter comes by and Bob asks the waiter if he can keep the bill to about $2.00 each. I thought I am going to like this job. It wasn't until years later that I learned the restaurant had betting games going on down stairs and what better cover than to have all these cops sitting in the restaurant.

* * *

It wasn't too long after getting into Traffic that my second wife and I decided that if there is such a thing as a blissful married life, it isn't with each other, and we separated. Our separating had nothing to do with the job but it is a pretty common thing in the police world. I moved into a one bedroom suite in a high rise apartment at Imperial and Willingdon in Burnaby. One evening I am on the main floor at Marg and Jimmy Stevens suite. They managed the apartment building and Jimmy was the equipment manager for the Police Motorcycle Drill Team. As we are sitting at the kitchen table we see a couple of guys acting suspicious around the building. I go outside and I see the two guys coming up the driveway from the underground parking lot. I approach them and ask them what they're up to and they tell me where to go. I grab one guy and spin him around and I get his arm behind his back as the second guy starts coming towards me. I am walking backwards towards the apartment front door pulling my guy along and I tell the second guy to back off or I will break his friends arm. The guy I have hold of also tells his friend to back off as I guess he is feeling a little pain. I get the guy into the building and Jimmy calls the RCMP as the buddy stands by across the street waiting for his buddy. The Mounties arrive and take the guy away for questioning. Afterwards I thought it was pretty stupid of me to take these guys on alone but it was a reaction that you think people expect you to take charge. I should have called the Mounties first and just kept an eye on them.

* * *

Tom Ridgewell, a fellow Traffic Cop and I appear in Provincial Court on a related traffic matter. We both are wearing our motorcycle uniforms with dress tunics, ties and motorcycle boots. Instead of wearing our motorcycle helmets we are wearing our regular soft uniform hats. I am first on the stand and I give my evidence and then Tom takes the stand and gives his. Before being excused, the Judge tells Tom to never appear in his court room again dressed looking like a Nazi. Tom complained to the Chief at the time because this was our uniform but I don't know that Tom's complaint went anywhere. The Judge was well known to hate the police, lawyers and everyone in general; he was a real odd ball and made some crazy decisions.

It's a beautiful spring day and I am riding my motorcycle south on Howe Street, a three lane one way street, and as I'm approaching the intersection of Nelson and Howe the traffic is all backed up in all the lanes. I work my way through the intersection and there is a small car parked in the middle of the traffic lane closest to the east side curb. I pull my motorcycle in front of the car and dismount and approach the vehicle. The vehicle is empty but it has a courier sign on the side window. I look around and don't see anybody. I go and get a ticket book from my bike and I see a fellow inside a business called The Law Office and he seems to be looking at me as I am writing a ticket and I begin to think it's probably his car. Sure enough the guy exits the building and walks over to his illegally parked car and asks," What's the problem officer?" I replied "What's the problem? Your car is parked in the middle of the road and all the traffic on Howe Street is backed up." The guy tells me he is a courier and he was delivering something to The Law Office. There is an open gravel parking lot right beside the building with vacant spaces and some meter parking still available at the curb. I point this out and the guy says in an indignant manner, "I'm not paying for parking". I ask him for his Driver's License and he produces a license in the name of Ronald Moron. He is still quite annoyed that I am going to give him a ticket and I say "Your name sure suits you," and I give him the ticket and ride away. Within half an hour I am called into the Internal Investigation Unit as the guy complained that I made fun of his name. My mouth always got me into trouble.

* * *

In those days it was the Traffic Division that was responsible to operate the drinking driving road blocks. Road blocks were fairly costly to operate as to be effective you needed at least 10 members to manage it. The senior traffic members never liked doing the roadblocks as it was pretty boring asking the same questions over and over and it could get darn cold standing in the same spot for an hour or so. Being the junior guys, me and the other ducks from the motorcycle training session got stuck doing this job. We would set up a roadblock but the key spots were the side streets before the roadblock. We would go after the people who are turning off to avoid the vehicle check. Its Christmas season and we have set up a roadblock near the Fraser Arms Hotel in South Vancouver. I check a young fellow who appears to have had too much to drink and I have him step out of his car. The guy gets out and starts running. There I am running after this guy in my motorcycle boots, helmet and all. We run north across 70th Avenue and I'm not losing any distance but I'm not gaining on him either. The guy runs in between some houses and runs into a chicken wire fence. The fight was on but Al Turner caught up to us and put his big size 12 boot on the guys back and I was able to handcuff the guy. It was no big deal. No extra charges for avoiding arrest. No assaulting a Police Officer, I just charged him with impaired driving. The guy had been drinking and he used bad judgment in choosing to run. No real harm was done other than I got my uniform dirty rolling around in the back yard.

It was around this period that I decided that being in ERT Containment and being a motorcycle cop didn't go together so I resigned from ERT. My good buddy Larry Young was still in ERT though and loving it. I couldn't imagine anything being better than this job. Here I am, an old sun worshipper, cruising around on a beautiful motorcycle, short sleeve shirt and catching the rays and getting a sun tan at the same time. What could be better? Someone told me that when a patrol officer saw a nice looking girl he would go around the block to have another look at her. When a Motorcycle Cop saw a nice looking girl he went around the block so she could have another look at him. If that didn't get her attention you would turn the corner so hard you would lean the bike right over and scrape the floor boards creating a big spark display. We really thought we were something.

* * *

One day shift I am stopped facing south on Oak Street, a major traffic artery, as I have just given a ticket to a taxi driver. The taxi has just pulled away and I am facing north standing beside my motorcycle finishing my notes on the back of the taxi driver's ticket. I feel a brush against my right shoulder and it's some guy about 20 years old riding a 10 speed bike north in the south bound lane of Oak Street. The guy continues north and then west on 42nd Avenue. I get on my motorcycle and go west on 43rd Avenue as I want to give this guy a ticket for being on the wrong side of the road. As I continue west on 43rd Avenue I see the guy is now riding south in the west lane of Oak Street towards 43rd so I make a u-turn and go back to the mouth of the lane. I ask the guy to pull over and he tells me" Don't bother me." The guy continues west on 43rd up a slight hill and I pull up beside him again and I say" Pull over I want to talk to you". This time the guy says "Go to hell". I can't believe it. This is a kid with an attitude. We are riding side by side, him on his 10 speed and I on my big Harley and I try one more time getting him to pull over and again he says not to bother him. I reach over to push him off his bike but when I let go of the throttle my bike slows down. We both just miss hitting a parked car and he goes onto the sidewalk. I advise the radio operator that I'm after a cyclist who is now north on Selkirk. The guy then rides his bike in between some houses and he goes out of my sight. I park my motorcycle and run to the back of the house and I hear sirens in the distance coming my way. There is a small lap dog tied up at the foot of the back stairs barking and growling at me. The 6 foot 20 year old suspect comes to the back door with a pen and paper in his hand and he asks for my name. I tell him to shut the fucking dog up or I'll shoot it. I am getting frustrated with this guy and losing my temper. The constant din of police sirens can be heard and they are obviously getting close. Pete Forster is the first Motorcycle cop to arrive and after I briefly tell him what has happened he carries the kid's bike from the back to the front yard. With that the kid comes out the front door screaming at Pete and yelling "Mom, they've got my bike". There are now about 4 more motorcycle cops, and a Patrol Supervisor at the front of the house and the BC TV van has just arrived. This is beginning to look like a major international incident and all I wanted to do was give the kid a traffic ticket. The kid's mother eventually comes to the front door and asks me to come into the house as I am wanted on the phone. It is Sergeant Terry Blythe from Internal Investigation. He tells me he is familiar with this kid from a previous incident and the family just phoned Internal Investigation a few minutes ago. Sergeant Blythe tells me after the kid's last incident where the police officer was found at fault the kid may be getting overly confident and trying to set me up. It is decided to give the kid some tickets and a Promise to Appear in Court for obstructing a police officer as the scene is becoming a major incident and more television crews on the way. About three months later the kid submits a letter to Internal Investigation accusing me of not only knocking him off his bike, but that I came back and ran over him twice while he was lying on the road which of course was not true. The Detectives in Internal Investigation tried to find some independent witnesses to the incident without success. Internal investigation asks if I would be willing to take a polygraph in order to clear this up but it is strictly voluntary. I volunteered to take the polygraph and the RCMP had a member fly in from Vancouver Island.

Taking a polygraph is a totally unique experience. The process takes several hours and you are only asked 5 or 6 questions and they tell you what they are going to ask you. What I didn't know at the time was our whole conversation was being tape recorded which was significant. I take the test at the RCMP office on west 70th Ave in Vancouver and I am hooked up to wires to my arms and chest. The RCMP Investigator tells me that it is important to 'Cleanse your soul' of any underlying guilt in order to get a true result in the test. The investigator and I cleanse my soul with my admissions of lying to my Father about using his car or stealing a chocolate bar as a kid and then we get into the questions.

"Is your name Douglas Barker and employed by the Vancouver Police Department"?
"Yes" I reply.

"Were you working as a police officer on April 10th, 1980 at 12:10 pm?" "Yes".

"Did you give a traffic ticket to Harvey Haymer for riding his bike the wrong way on Oak Street?" "Yes".

"Did you run over Harvey Haymer with your motorcycle?" "No".

As the testing is in progress and I am watching the needle moving about on the polygraph paper recording my answers and I am hoping I have cleansed enough of my soul to satisfy the RCMP Investigator.

The suspect, Harvey Haymer had volunteered to take the polygraph as well by the Vancouver Investigator, Detective Vince Falcon. Several weeks later Vince told me that the suspect failed the polygraph and the RCMP concluded that I was telling the truth.

When I first became a policeman and I would get called to court, I would give my evidence and then sit in the back of the public area of the court and wait for the outcome of the trial. I think this practice may have been frowned upon by some Judges as it looked as if you were too eager for a guilty verdict. Since then I would normally give my evidence and when I was excused by the Judge I would leave the Court House. Heck, I had better things to do than sit in the courtroom and listen to a lawyer explain that his poor client is like this because he was abused as a child or it's the fault of the Social System. This case was different, it was personal and I was going to sit through every minute as I wanted to see some revenge for the outlandish accusations that had been made and the many sleepless nights.

Over the next year there are several court appearances with the first being in Traffic Court and the kid is found guilty of the traffic offences. Then we go to criminal court for Obstructing a Police Officer. I take the stand and give my evidence in chief and I am cross examined by the defendant's lawyer. The trial is going to a second day and Harvey tells the Judge he can't make it that day because he has to study for final exams at UBC. The Judge loses it and explains the facts to Harvey that he had better be in court or he will be arrested and facing serious charges. The next day the case continues and the Prosecutor is asking Harvey questions when Harvey states he took a polygraph test by the Vancouver Police Department. I think 'aha', the truth will come out. The Prosecutor never asks Harvey what the result of his test was but goes on to another question. At the conclusion of the trial the judge finds Harvey guilty of Obstruction, case closed. The court case made the front page of the Province and Sun newspapers. SEVEN OFFICERS GET THEIR MAN. ONE CYCLIST and the paper proceeded to name names. The news paper headlines and the article I'm sure was intended to make the 'cops' look stupid and they probably achieved that. I won the Traffic case and the Criminal case but I wanted to sue the kid and his family. Crown Counsel and the Police Union wouldn't go along with it as they thought the kid had had enough. I was bitter as I had gone through a year and a half of sleepless nights thinking about people believing the kid and the criticism from my work mates for volunteering in taking the polygraph in the first place. I told the Department that that is the last time I will ever take a polygraph if that is the support you get.

* * *

I have been in traffic long enough that I can order my own motorcycle boots where they are made to measure for me and I don't have to wear hand me downs. I am down at the shoemakers near Broadway and Alma with Al Turner being measured for new boots. The shoemaker is Italian and makes his own home made wine. As is the case of all home brewers he naturally wants us to sample the quality of his product. The shoemaker offers us a glass of wine and we accept but then that leads to another. I don't want to insult him because he is making me a brand new pair of leather boots you know and I want them to fit. We start riding our bikes back towards downtown when the alarm sounds on the police radio. There has been a bank robbery and we are going code 3, lights and siren on east on Point Grey Road when an elderly lady backs her car out of her driveway. Al swerves to miss her but he just catches her rear bumper. Al and his bike go down and they continue sliding into the oncoming traffic and both Al and his bike go under a commercial truck. I was on the radio calling for an ambulance, fire, a supervisor and everything they have. Al dusted himself off and cancelled everyone but the Supervisor hoping he wouldn't smell the wine. I have seen Alex MacDonald crash and now Turner. I wonder to myself when is it going to be my turn?

* * *

I have my first encounter with Linda the tit lady, a woman about 25 years old, very attractive with a huge chest and she seemed to hang around the Granville and Davie area or the Granville Street Bridge. I had pulled over a violator on the north side of the Granville Bridge on my motorcycle and I'm in the process of writing the ticket, standing beside my bike that still has the emergency lights going, the red and yellow flashing lights on the front and the blue tear drop light on the back fender. This woman comes up to me and asks "Can I touch it?" I am wondering what she is talking about. I said "Can you touch what?" "Can I touch the titty?" she says pointing at the blue flashing tear drop light on the fender. I'm a little embarrassed and wonder what the violator is thinking but I say ok to which she starts fondling the light. It turns out she is a lesbian who is fixated with these lights that are the shape of a woman's breast and has been stopping police officers on motorcycles or unmarked police cars with similar dash lights for some time. I had two other encounters with her. She was harmless but strange.

* * *

It's Saturday night in the middle of July 1980. The Sea Festival, an annual event held at English Bay in the West End, has begun and the festivities started with a parade that morning along Beach Avenue. The Motor Cycle Drill Team, all being members of the Traffic Division, performed in the parade and are now partying some place in town. The Sea Festival has had problems over the past couple of years with rowdies and drunks and it seems to get worse every year. There is a lot of drinking on the beach and a salmon barbeque. By 11 pm things are usually pretty active down there.

Because the Drill Team members are not working tonight, there are only about 6 or 7 of our Traffic Squad members working. We are having dinner in the back kitchen at Puccini's Restaurant on Main Street when The Chief Dispatcher calls Sergeant Dave Zurr. The CD tells Dave to have the traffic members stay close to

English Bay later in the evening in case of problems. About 11:30 pm the radio operator calls us to head to the beach as problems are starting. When we arrive the Fire Department is there as some idiot started a fire in one of the large commercial garbage containers and when the firemen tried to put the fire out, people started throwing things at them. We parked our motorcycles in a safe area from the crowd and we were handed a riot stick and told we would be clearing the beach. There were probably 15 to 20 Patrol members from District 1 and they were given proper riot equipment with helmets, face shields and riot sticks. Everyone spread across the beach from the side walk near the road to the waters edge. The traffic guys were mostly near the water. The Superintendent in charge was sitting in a police car, on the beach but closest to the road, and was to give the official riot warning for the crowd to disperse. He hadn't said anything yet and the rocks and empty bottles started flying at the lined up police officers. I am getting pretty nervous because there are probably 3,000 people still at the beach and there are about 25 police officers. I look to my left and about 8 officers away I see Gordy Corson who had been a traffic instructor when I was first in the Academy and had been transferred back to Patrol recently. I think he has to be close to 55 years old and I think he shouldn't have to be putting up with this shit. The rocks and bottles are hard to see in the darkness and are still flying our way. The guys with shields will block them and the rest of us kind of bob and weave like prize fighters avoiding a punch. I look behind as a bottle just went flying over my head and I see a large crowd gathering behind us, collecting the previously thrown bottles. We are in trouble. The Superintendent starts to slowly make his speech over the loud hailer and the bottles fly even more. While the Superintendent was still talking on the loud hailer, a police officer tired of being hit by flying debris and the Superintendants lengthy warning to the crowd, yelled "Charge", and we did.

We rushed the crowd and started flailing away with our night sticks. We came upon a couple still sitting on a blanket sharing a bottle of wine and we told them to leave. The guy starts to argue and tell us he has the right to stay there, that it's a free country. That's all I want to do in the middle of a riot is get into a debate.

He was given a swift prod with a night stick and they moved. The crowd started to break up with the regular citizens, who had been enjoying the rock and bottle show, now fearing for their lives decided to get the hell out of there. That left several hundred assholes that had broken up into smaller groups. We forged ahead with one group at a time and I can say no mercy was given. There would be an arrest team behind us and you would get a guy or girl and turn them over to the arrest team and get back into action. The action lasted several hours. These thugs had this riot previously planned as they had rocks stored away in various hiding places to be used later in the night. After clearing the beach we started to move up Denman Street and continue fighting. There was a large crowd at a small park near Morton and Denman and I saw Dave Zurr tell a guy who was drinking a bottle of beer to put his beer bottle down. The guy didn't and Dave gave him a good swat on the hand with his riot stick. The bottle dropped and then there were a lot of tears.

I was standing behind a building at Morton and Denman and I stuck my head around the corner and wham, I got hit by a big chunk of broken asphalt in my right collar bone. I hit the ground like Sonny Liston. Al Turner helped me get up and a couple of moments later I saw a guy hiding behind a VW Beetle on the other side of Denman. The guy would stand up and throw something at the police and then duck down again behind the car. I thought this is probably the guy that just got me and I see red. I run across Denman and the guy behind the VW sees me coming and runs north on the east sidewalk. Even in my motorcycle boots and helmet I am gaining on him and swinging but missing with my long riot stick. After about a block of running, the guy makes a mistake and turns right to go east on Comox Street. It's a mistake because I am right handed and he has just got into my swing reach. I hit him with a glancing blow on the right side of his head and he goes down hard and I actually run by him and have to come back. The paddy wagon is right there and as I put the guy in the back I lose it and give him a good fist in the nose. It was not professional I know but circumstances were heated and adrenalin was running high. Things were calming down with only a few skirmishes left. It's about 2:30 am and The Century Plaza Hotel on Burrard Street is on fire and the Traffic members are told to leave the riot and go and direct traffic at the fire. While we were there we run into some of the combatants from the riot that are going to St. Paul's Hospital for treatment which is next door to the hotel. We had a good laugh. We return to the police garage about 3:30 am, well past our shift, and have a beer in the garage and compare war stories. We hear some noise outside the police garage and there is some guy breaking into Robin Boyer's personal car that's parked on the street. Robin took care of that and arrested the guy. What a night. I think to myself that I should join the Drill Team so I don't have to do this again next year.

* * *

The entire Police Department was into Team Policing in those days, a new concept where the police worked closely with the community and social workers. This new concept meant that because of the many new shift times a few of the officers never saw each other to compare notes and exchange information on activities in their jurisdiction, so every 3 or 4 months the Police Team would have a Team Training Day. Traffic decided we would have Team Training Days as well but they usually led to a disaster. I lost 2 pay cheques playing cards at different Team Training Days and I was lucky I was living alone. Another time we decided to go on a pub crawl and ended up at the Main Hotel. We were off duty and one of the guys decides to ride his personal motorcycle into the bar and as he comes crashing through the front doors, he rides up to the bar and asks for a beer. It was some time later that we learned there had been a major investigation going on at this bar for stolen property involving some other police officers and there were surveillance cameras throughout the place. Our antics were small potatoes for what had been going on there and nothing happened to us. The Main Hotel investigation did result in a number of officers being fired from the force.

* * *

It's been a beautiful day on a long weekend and there isn't much in the way of traffic problems. The Corporal wants me to go get some ice after we had done a motorcycle escort so we can have a few drinks in the police garage before we go home. I am driving north on the old Cambie Street swing bridge and I pull a car over for speeding. We are on the middle of the bridge and it turns out the driver is wanted on some outstanding traffic warrants and I arrest him. I have to wait for the police wagon to take him away and a tow truck to move the car off the bridge. It's a warm day and I can see water dripping from my saddle bags as the ice is melting. The boss keeps coming on the air and asking the operator "Where is motorcycle 966?" Corporal Bob Delf is the nicest guy and I have never seen him get mad at any of the guys but he was furious with me this day. It turned out not only did I have the melting ice but I also had the cork screw to open the bottles of wine.

* * *

There had been lots of problems with prostitutes working in the residential area of the West End around Davie and Jarvis Street. The prostitutes were hanging out on the street corners and the laneways until 4am and the neighborhood is tired of the continual traffic and noise from the lanes. The Traffic Division is instructed to harass the drivers of these vehicles by ticketing them for every minor infraction in order to discourage them from coming in to the area. One evening around midnight I observe a car pull up and pick up a known transvestite in the north lane of Davie Street and I give pursuit. I stop the vehicle around the beach at English Bay and ask the driver and his passenger for identification which they provide. I know the passenger is Jack Brusso as I checked him the night before and I decide to have some fun. I say "Hello Jack" to the passenger and ask the driver if he makes it a habit of picking up other men. The driver is horrified as Jack is looking very attractive as a woman and smartly dressed in an expensive looking leopard skin full length coat. I write the driver a ticket for no front license plate and then tell him his name could be forwarded to the Sexual Offence Squad as a pervert but if he promises to never return to the area I will let it go. The driver, a married man, promises to never return and kicks Jack out of the car and drives away. The late night hooker problem lasted about a month and they finally moved on to another area.

* * *

One afternoon shift we have just started work and we meet at the back of Puccini's Restaurant for dinner. There are about four of us including Corporal Bob Delf. Sergeant Dave Zurr is late because he had a promotional interview for the S/Sgt rank. Dave arrives and sits down but he looks depressed. We asked him how the interview went and he said not well. Dave says "They said, Zurr; you run your shift like a country club". We all laughed but Dave didn't. He was a smart guy with a degree in Education and he had had his fun on the job but now he wanted to get promoted again. The owner of the restaurant approached us and Bob, the Corporal, ordered a bottle of wine with dinner. Dave was furious and said no way. Bob laughed and said "Who do you think is running this shift Dave? You don't have to have any if you don't want to." Dave had had a bad day already and decided to have some wine to calm him down. When Bob was with us at Puccini's we usually rolled the poker dice with the owner, double or nothing for the bill. We always won it seemed, but when Bob got transferred we never won again and had to pay double the price. We didn't go there as often after that. Both Bob and Dave were transferred soon after this dinner.

The Vancouver Police Union had purchased some land and built a 6 storey office building around 1978 at 190 Alexander Street. The building had the Vancouver Police Credit Union and the Vancouver Police Union office on the main floor and then a lot of law offices through out the building. On the top floor was the Police Club. This was a beautiful bar with a dance floor, pool table and a great view over Burrard Inlet. On a Thursday or Friday night this was as busy as any other night club in town but it was a safe haven where the police officers could cut loose without mixing with the criminal element at a regular establishment. Up until this time the police officers as well as some Judges, Prosecutors and Defense Counsel would drink and mingle in the back room of the Empress Hotel which was anything but a classy bar but was conveniently located right behind the police station and close to the Provincial Courts. The Police Club would eventually close in the mid 1990's when the 10 hour day is brought in and members worked until at least 2 am past the club operating hours.

* * *

In October 1980 there were some vacancies coming available for the Motorcycle Drill Team and I was invited to join. I had just met what was soon to be Mrs. Barker the Third and as she met me at a Motorcycle Drill Team event, I wasn't sure how she was going to accept my being part of this carousing group. The Motorcycle Drill Team was originally formed in 1954 and they really did do some tricky stuff back then, like 3 or 4 guys on one motorcycle and doing hand stands as the bike is moving. That all stopped when the Workers Compensation Board said they would not cover them if they had an accident. As a member of the Drill Team you are required to practice every Wednesday afternoon during the spring and summer months. If you are working you go to practice. If it's your day off, you are required to come in and go to practice on your own time. The Drill Team performs in many local parades but usually you get one good invitation each year to something special like the Calgary Stampede or Palm Springs with most of the expenses being paid by a benefactor, and your time by the Police Department.

It is the end of May 1981 and we have been practicing our maneuvers at the PNE parking lot for several months and performed at a couple of small events. We are requested to do a performance as the half time show at the Vancouver Whitecaps soccer game held at Empire Stadium. While the first half of the game is being played, we are invited by one of the local breweries to sit in their hospitality room and have a beer. There isn't enough room on the oval track for all the bikes to perform so Don MacLaren and I, being the junior members on the team stay in the hospitality suite and drink beer as the other guys do the performance. As the Team is riding around the track one of the 15,000 fans in attendance throws a chunk of ice and hits Al Hutton in the head injuring him. Al has been the teams split bike in our performances this year and he's now off work for a few weeks.

The team needs a volunteer to be the split bike for the up and coming West Vancouver parade.

The Wednesday practice arrives and I volunteer to be the split bike. There are two split maneuvers, the single split and the double split. The single split is performed at a lower speed than the double but a little more dangerous. In this maneuver the split bike drives head on at the other 7 motorcycles that are single file and approaching from the opposite direction. The 7 approaching bikes are to break off as the split bike approaches, alternating one to the left and one to the right and so on. Other than the lead rider, no one can see the split bike coming until the rider ahead has broken off to the left or right and there he is. The closing speed is about 100 km/h as the split bike is doing 60 km/h and the other approaching 7 bikes are doing 40 km/h. We practice the entire routine including the single split which is the second of all the maneuvers and there are no problems.

Saturday, June 6, 1981 and it's my day in more ways than one. I am going to be the star of the show, the split bike. The team rides in formation from Vancouver and across the Lions Gate Bridge into West Vancouver where we go for a pre parade breakfast. Jim and Marg Stevens have always been our designated equipment managers and Jim as usual brought along some special pre ride orange juice to calm the nerves. As we are having breakfast Larry Holbrook, the riding Corporal and Pete Forster were giving me a hard time about waiting until the last second to split off in the single split but I shook it off.

The parade starts from Ambleside Park and we start off moving west on Marine Drive with a crowd of spectators sitting or standing at the curbs edge. Larry Holbrook blows the whistle and we move into a straight line formation across the road. He blows the whistle again, breaking off that formation and leading to the single split. This is my key to leave the group and head back to approach the group head on. I turn back towards Ambleside Park and when I get there I make a u-turn to approach the oncoming team. I speed up to about 60 km/h and I don't see the team yet as I have a curve in the road ahead of me. As I get around the curve there they are and I am up to Holbrook, the first bike. Larry always likes to wait until the last second to break off. That's fine for him but the guy behind doesn't have much time to react. Larry breaks left towards the curb then Pete Forster breaks right towards the right curb. Don Stark breaks left, Doug Lacey breaks right, John Wobick breaks left, and then there is a problem. Don MacLaren is breaking right but he is steering to the right and not leaning the bike over. I hit the left side saddle bag of Don's bike with my left front crash guard and then my bike brushes off the right side of the next bike that is breaking left ridden by Dave Clark. I have my siren on and I'm beginning to feel some pain from my left foot. I look down and I see that my left crash bar has broken off and gone through my left foot. I slow down, turn the siren off and start to think what I'm going to do. The rest of the team is way behind me and going in the opposite direction and other than Don and Dave, the team doesn't know what has happened. I didn't fall. I'm still going west on Marine Drive and the pain in my foot is getting unbearable. I am slowing down and I can tell that the crowd knows something is wrong now. I see my old classmate from the Academy, Lou Williams, in the crowd and we make eye contact. He knows something is wrong and he and a West Vancouver Police Officer gesture me over to the right curb. I turn off my bike and coast towards them with the clutch in. I can't move my left foot to be able to change the gear to neutral. As I slowly glide to a stop the police officer holds the bike as Lou Williams lifts me off the bike and places me on to the ground.

This is my day alright and here I am, the star of the parade, lying on the pavement with some lady holding my left hand, Pete Forster having caught up to me now holding my right and the firemen cutting off my brand new pair of boots with a knife. A Doctor from the crowd looked at my foot and said I would need an operation. He asked if I had been drinking and would I take a Breathalyzer test. I said no thanks. I wondered if he smelled the special orange juice or was it that he thought anyone who would do such a stupid maneuver like that must have been drinking. Dave Clark phoned my wife at home and told her about the accident and that it didn't look good for me. Fortunately the Sergeant, Chuck Dennis, took the phone from Dave and said it was no big deal.

After about 15 minutes the ambulance arrives and they tell me they are going to take me to the Lions Gate Hospital in North Vancouver. I realize no one will ever visit me over there and I talk them into taking me to St. Paul's Hospital in Vancouver as well as allowing me to have a couple of smokes in the ambulance on the way there.

I remember being in the emergency ward and the ambulance attendants wouldn't leave the hospital until they had seen my foot. I was wheeled out into the hallway where I remained for an hour before a nurse asked if I had received anything for pain. After I replied no, they gave me a shot of morphine and then everything seemed wonderful. I remember my Dad looking at my foot in the emergency ward when I finally got a bed and saying "That looks nasty." In all this time I hadn't seen my foot and I didn't want to. I just wanted everything to be normal again.

I was operated on that night as I had a bone missing in my foot and the Doctor had to take a piece from my right hip and put it in my left foot. It was all held together with an 18 inch spike that exited out my left big toe and it had a rubber bumper at the end. At least now I had a reason for the nick name Spike. I don't think Donny MacLaren ever felt comfortable on the motorcycle but he loved to party and Traffic was the place to be.

I was on crutches for 4 months and off work for a total of 6 months and ended up going to Workers Compensation for rehabilitation, which meant building wishing wells as part of my therapy. That alone made me better; I wanted to get the hell out of there.

I returned to work and spent the first couple of weeks riding around with the training instructor to make sure I could still ride and with no fear. Everything was fine although it's December and lousy weather. I learned that my old partner from Team 31, Barry McKew had been fired with a couple of other policemen for having some involvement in B&E's and stolen property. This was not the Main Hotel but something entirely different. I was pretty disappointed in Barry but we didn't need guys like this on the job.

* * *

January 1982 Al Turner and I are working afternoon shift using an unmarked police car because of the inclement weather. It's my first day of trying to quit smoking cigarettes and so far so good. The radio operator calls and asks if we would change channels and go to channel 4 as there has been a hostage taking and they need traffic control in the area. We change channels and are requested to attend at 10th and Birch. We block off the intersection as requested and sit back and relax. Apparently some guy has taken a young girl hostage and is holed up in an apartment building on the south side of the 1300 block of West 10th Avenue. This situation had been going on for about an hour before we got there. The Emergency Response Team has been called to attend and a hostage negotiator and a Command Post had been set up nearby.

The situation as always drags on into the night and someone has gone and got everyone Big Mac hamburgers from the nearest McDonalds Restaurant.

The events are starting to get a little more hectic as the suspect has threatened to cut off one of the hostage's fingers. A short time later some police officer comes and knocks on the closed passenger window of our car and being the passenger I open the window. The officer says they are looking for someone to volunteer to drive a van. I thought ah ha, more hamburgers. I said I would help them out and left the police car and followed the other officer expecting to get instructions on how many burgers to pick up at the local McDonalds. He led me to the Command Post. They actually wanted me to drive the Hostage Taker's van. It turns out one of the suspect's demands for releasing the hostage is having his van being delivered to him. He thinks he is a bit of a race car driver and if he gets his van delivered to him, he will be able to get away and elude capture. The officer in charge says as part of the negotiation I should drive the van to the corner of Hemlock Street and west 10th where the suspect will be able to see his van. I do this and then drive the van back to the Command Post and go inside. The Command Post is trying to formulate a plan of attack and asks me how I feel about changing places with the hostage. I tell them I don't feel really good about it and ask if anyone has a cigarette. I have a smoke and then the suggestion is made that I drive the van with Bob McGee, an ERT member, in the back of the van and after I leave the van and the suspect gets behind the wheel Bob will shoot the guy. Good, now we have a dead suspect and a runaway van with an ERT member in the back. Back to the thinking chair. The suspect is getting impatient and I wouldn't mind another smoke, of course I don't have any, I'm a non smoker or at least I was.

It's decided I will drive the van to the front door of the apartment building and stop the van precisely when I am told to. I will exit the van leaving the engine running with the driver's door open and run like hell away from there. Someone gives me another cigarette and they strap the large 50 pound bullet proof vest on me over my motorcycle uniform. I drive the van to the corner of 10th and Birch and wait for instructions to slowly move in. At this point I remove my Smith & Wesson .38 revolver from my holster and place the gun on the dash of the van in case I may need it.

I am waiting for what seems an eternity for the instruction to move in and I notice the van's gas gauge is reading empty. I advise the Command Post of the gas situation and that we better hurry up. They give me the command to begin moving but to drive slowly and stop exactly when they say. I begin going west on 10th Avenue with one hand on the wheel and the other on my gun on the dash. The command is given to stop and I put the vehicle in park, get my gun and start running east on the south side walk wearing a 50 pound bullet proof vest and motorcycle boots. I get to a building to the east of the suspect's building and I start to duck into a darkened area when a blackened face appears and an ERT member in his battle fatigues says "Get the hell out of here Barker". It is 4am and everything is deathly quiet. I hear the suspect open the door of his building and he starts to run for the waiting van. I hear someone yell "Stop or I'll shoot". I run a little further east and hide behind a parked car as I'm anticipating some action. The suspect has just got into the van when a shot is fired and there is a spark at one of the suspect's vehicle wheels. A police officer yells "he's shooting back" and all hell breaks loose.

It sounds like Vietnam or the Fourth of July celebration. The van is literally rocking from side to side and you can hear the zinging of bullets hitting metal. It seemed like it went on for several minutes but I honestly have no idea. Someone yelled to cease fire and it was dead silent with the exception of the hissing of tires losing their air from bullet holes. Like the end of a fireworks display, the air was full of smoke. I thought this guy has to be toast; the van has to be full of holes. I saw it with my own eyes. Then a moaning started. It was coming from inside the van and I couldn't believe it. Someone yelled "Come out and you won't get hurt." I started laughing quietly to myself. Then someone yelled "Reach for the sky". I thought we have to get some new lines for our ERT members. It was all over. The suspect limped out of the van with a minor ankle injury and was arrested. The neighborhood and its parked cars were full of holes. There were well over 60 rounds fired, some were shot guns with SSG shot and some were AR 15's where someone emptied their weapon and reloaded. Unfortunately the Chief Constable, Bob Stewart wasn't advised of the correct number of rounds fired as he advised the morning press meeting that there were only two shots fired. The noon news ran his morning statement then they showed the actual footage. They had filmed the entire shooting quite accurately including the reach for the sky comments.

Everyone involved had to attend a debriefing immediately after the incident and when it was over I went to my boss to take the next night off as I needed the sleep. He said ok and that he was putting me up for a Chief Constables Commendation, the highest commendation you can receive, for volunteering to drive the van in this dangerous incident. The next day when I arrived for work, I was told I would only get an Inspectors Commendation because as it turned out the suspect never really had a knife or a gun. Had I known that, I wouldn't have had to wear the bullet proof vest when I drove the van and I would have let him take me hostage. Remember, common sense. Sometimes things are pretty stupid but you have to laugh. The Canadian Police College in Ottawa had the news clip and used it in one of the courses I attended. Oh, I started smoking again after that incident.

* * *

Since Dave Zurr and Bob Delf have been transferred to other
duties, we have had an entire new group of leaders from the
Corporal up to the Inspector. They are going to be cleaning house
and removing these free spirits in the Traffic Division. The new
Sergeant is John Friesen a no nonsense guy who openly has plans
of climbing up the promotional ladder as fast as he can and a brand
new Corporal Ken Doherty. Ken had been a constable in traffic on
our shift and yet they brought him back right after getting
promoted. Ken may not have been the level of trouble maker as
the rest of us but he had his skeletons as well. He was put in a
tough situation now having to clean up the mess he was part of at
one time. We were bad. I think there was some resentment from
Patrol members who had weekly inspections and they were
responsible for answering to all kinds of boring calls. The traffic
guys got away with long hair hidden under their helmets, lots of
overtime from court and movie call outs and were seldom called
for on the radio. There was no midnight shift and it was easy to
hide or get in trouble.

After six months I am back on the Motorcycle Drill Team but *I
would like a little more room please"*. Practice commences for the
1982 summer season.

It's a sunny Spring Saturday and the traffic members meet in the
office. The Sergeant, John Friesen advises that we will be
attending a bed race at the Granville Mall. The race has been
promoted by the various local media and they have requested our
assistance in blocking off streets and traffic control. In the mean
time the Sergeant suggests if we are going to have breakfast we
should do it now.

For some reason my motorcycle was left in the basement at
Headquarters by my riding partner and not in the Police Garage on
Powell Street. I exit the downstairs parking lot at Headquarters
and start riding west on Powell as I'm going to meet some guys for
breakfast in the West End. As I am approaching Main Street I hear
the emergency beep tone on the radio and the radio operator

talking about a robbery that had occurred around the 500 block Powell Street. I stop at a red light at Main Street and a transit bus pulls up beside me. The driver is waving his hands and saying something that I can't make out over the sound of my motorcycle. I pull over in front of the bus and turn my bike off. The bus driver opens the passenger doors of the bus and tells me there are 2 women and a man walking this way that seemed to be having some kind of a fight several blocks back. These 3 people have just approached Main Street as I am talking to the bus driver. I am not sure yet what is going on but I start talking to the three people and ask for some identification. As I'm talking to them I hear the radio operator describe one of the male suspects in the robbery as having dark collar length hair and wearing an Indian sweater. One of the females I am talking to has dark collar length hair and is wearing an Indian sweater. No sooner do I advise the operator I may be with the suspects when Carl Havdale appears from behind the one wearing the Indian sweater and yells "What's this?" Carl holds up a large Bowie knife that the female was holding behind her back. With that I reach down the top of her Indian sweater and pull out a brown bag that contained $240 cash. The male was not involved but only a witness to the robbery and the two females were arrested. Patrol units attended and their Sergeant, Al Grandia, were very happy about the arrest. Carl and I now had several hours of reports to do and our Traffic Sergeant John Friesen was furious. John Friesen asked us "What are you doing getting involved in a Patrol case when you knew we had a bed race about to begin?" There it is again, the 95% common sense. Al Grandia just laughed about our Sergeant's comments and said "Some people can't handle the pressure of high command." How true. Carl and I did receive an Inspector's Commendation from our Traffic Sergeant who I think was trying to cover his tracks when he realized how ridiculous his comments were.

Carl told me a few weeks later when he and John Friesen were walking towards the Police Garage that day to get their motorcycles they saw me talking to the suspects on the north east corner of Main and Powell. Carl said to John that the person in the Indian sweater is holding a knife behind their back and he crossed the street to assist me. Apparently John Friesen replied to Carl that he would see him later and kept on walking to the Police Garage choosing not to get involved.

I wasn't very happy about my Sergeant's actions that day. He owned a very nice 1981 Firebird with all the bells and whistles. He was working the 6pm to 2am shift a few weeks later and I put an Ad in the newspaper to sell his car at about $3,000 under the normal value. At the end of the Ad I said ask for John and call before 7am. In those days you only had to provide a phone number to place an ad and of course, the newspaper sent him the bill.

* * *

I am back on the Drill Team but I'm not the split bike. Doug Lacey is the split bike and Al Hutton is the riding Corporal this year. We did implement a new move called the triple split and I volunteered for that. In this move you had 2 split bikes going head on at the other 6. It was a crowd pleaser. The closing speed was about 160 km/h. In hind sight it was getting a little dangerous. We felt comfortable, but looking back at tapes of some of those parades there are people crossing from one side of the street to the other as we're approaching and we wouldn't have a chance to avoid someone. It would have been bad, not just for us, but the spectators as well. The main ride this year was the Calgary Stampede and then we did the usual Seattle, PNE and Port Alberni parades. In order to get to the Calgary Stampede we needed some financial assistance generously offered by a local businessman Joe Cohen. Mr. Cohen had always been very pro police and helped out the Police Pipe Band and Drill Team before. As I recall he gave the team $7500 to defer our costs and to use as we saw fit. At the end of the Drill Team season the Superintendant for the Traffic Division said all the members had to repay their portion of the $7500 donation that was used for airfare and hotel to the Motor Cycle Drill Team bank account. This would have been about $250 each and there was an uprising causing almost everyone to quit the team. It wasn't handled very well by either side I think we thought you would never get another Drill Team. A new Drill Team was formed from scratch with new members the next year.

The new Team may not have been as good at first but in no time it was up to speed and maybe better. The Motorcycle Drill Team is still active today.

* * *

We did our job but there is no doubt we pushed the limit and did a lot of stupid things. It was the September long week end in 1982 and we had given out our 20 tickets and another Traffic member and I went to a friend of his around 13th and Cambie Street. I had just bought a house the day before so we celebrated with a couple of drinks and then I left alone to go back to the office. On the way back I stopped at a grocery store and purchased a pack of cigarettes. I returned to the office and spoke to the acting Corporal Phil Bromly, a very no nonsense guy, as we waited for the rest of the shift to come in. I spoke to Phil for about 45 minutes about the house I bought and then I went home.

Two days later after my days off, we were having our daily meeting before hitting the streets and Bill Walden, the Corporal, asks "Who was the blonde motorcycle cop with a blonde moustache, photo grey sunglasses, and was drunk and staggered out of a grocery store at 13th and Cambie on Monday afternoon?" I knew he was referring to me as I looked at the work sheets for Monday and advise "Bill, I am the only guy that fits that description, and in fact I was in the grocery store but I hadn't been drinking. I walk with a bit of a limp after my motorcycle accident last year."

Apparently two women were in the store when I bought my smokes and complained to the store owner about smelling liquor on the policemen's breath and then they called Headquarters. I had already gone home. The investigation went on for quite some time but it was eventually dropped when the store owner said he didn't smell anything and I seemed quite normal. Phil Bromly advised he has done hundreds of impaired drivers and Barker seemed sober. End of story. I was lucky and it was time to smarten up.

* * *

No one ever said "Gee thanks for the ticket, I deserved that." Everyone was innocent or wanted a break. A speeder would say "Why don't you catch a bank robber" and later on in my career when I caught bank robbers they would say "Why don't you catch some speeders." You could never win. While I hated writing tickets in patrol, in Traffic it grew on you. You became ruthless because you have heard every excuse in the book and you just wanted your 20 tickets. I gave tickets to TV personalities, Vancouver Canuck Hockey players, four Nuns and even politicians. Every time it was the same. "Don't you know who I am", or "Can't you give me a break?" After four years it became tiresome unless it was a good red light or someone doing 30 km/h over the speed limit. When someone really became a jerk or argumentative it became fun and enjoyable. They would say "I'll see you in court and I hope it's your day off". We hoped that too because we got eight hours pay for a fifteen minute appearance on our days off.

* * *

I had just started my shift one night around 6pm and I stop this business tycoon driving a beautiful new big Mercedes Benz at Georgia and Thurlow Street. I asked the driver for his license and explained he had a front head light burnt out. The driver gave me his license and thanked me for telling him about the headlight and he would get it fixed. Like a fisherman and this being the first catch of the day, I'm not prepared to throw this one back not knowing what the rest of the day may bring. I give the driver the ticket for the one headlight and he lets into me. "I guess this ticket makes your quota" he yells at me. I responded in a very calm voice and said "No sir, I've already made my quota; this ticket is for the beginning of next months quota". Within 20 minutes the Traffic Corporal Bill Walden calls me on the air and tells me to get into the Traffic Office. I get to the office and Walden asks if I told this guy we had a quota and I say yes I did. "How can you be so stupid"? Walden yells at me. "We do have a quota Bill because 2 guys just got transferred for not writing enough tickets" I replied. "We have a reasonable level of production for a days pay, not a quota" Bill says. So from then on we called it RELP and not a quota. I hate to say it but I think I enjoyed pissing people off sometimes.

* * *

It was raining one day and I was working radar out of an unmarked police car on west 16th Avenue and I pulled over a car for speeding. I approached the driver and got his driver's licence and returned to my car to fill out the ticket. I noticed that the driver was a notable provincial politician but I continued writing the ticket. The passenger door of the speeding car opened and an older woman walks over to my drivers window and asks "Don't you know who that is?" I said "Yes Maam," and I pointed at the individual's name on the driver's license and repeated the driver's name," It says so right here on his drivers license" and I continued writing the ticket. The lady returned to their car in a huff but the politician never said anything. Sometimes your passenger isn't doing you any favors. The politician was influential enough he could have had the ticket cancelled and he probably did.

If you gave a break to everyone you would never give out a ticket and you would be looking for work. People didn't just get tickets for speeding. There were U-turns, crosswalks, J-walking, no front plate, unsafe lane change, obstructed vision (radar detector). The list was endless.

* * *

I was watching a stop sign in front of the old rugby house where I lived when I first joined the job. The corner of MacDonald and Point Grey Road was famous for people rolling through the stop sign without stopping. I saw a small car roll through the stop sign and continue east on Point Grey Road. I pulled the car over and it contained four Nuns. I told them why I stopped them and they said they slowed down before they made the turn. I gave them a ticket for failing to stop at a traffic control device. It reminded me of the joke of the policeman in court after the accused said he slowed down for the stop sign and the policeman asked if he started punching the man in the face did he want him to stop hitting him or just slow down

* * *

Remembering that the job is 95% commonsense, I recall that mine may have been absent this one afternoon. I was watching an intersection at 6th and Cambie waiting for someone to turn against the no left turn sign. It was cold out and I was hiding behind a large billboard sign with my engine running and warming my hands near the motorcycle's engine. I had a ticket already written with the date, location and the offence. All I needed was a victim and their name to put on the ticket and then I could meet the guys for dinner in the next fifteen minutes. A car turns left and pulls into the Chevron gas station. I have my victim and I put my bike in gear and ride over to the vehicle where a very nice lady about 30 years old is exiting her car. I advise the lady why I am there and that she turned against a no left turn sign. The lady explains she realizes that but she has a flat tire and needed to get some air. I look and sure enough her back left tire is going flat. She is all dressed up so I take the air hose and fill up her tire for her. Because I already have the ticket half completed I give her the ticket anyway and I am on my way to dinner. I was a real asshole and had lost touch with reality and common sense. That is the only ticket I ever felt bad about. I got a court notice for Traffic Court and there was the lady. I felt stupid all over again and told the judge I had no evidence having lost the ticket and the case was thrown out. I knew the time was getting close for me to leave traffic.

* * *

One of the enjoyable functions in traffic was doing motorcycle escorts for various dignitaries and VIP's. In the spring of 1983 Her Majesty Queen Elizabeth and Prince Philip visited Vancouver and we spent three days escorting them around the city. At the end of the tour we lead them to the airport where the Queen and Prince Philip spoke to each of us personally. There were only about twelve of us but because we would leap frog the motorcade and there was always someone at an intersection when their car went through, Philip's perception was that there were a great many more policemen assigned to the team. It was fun.

In the fall of 1983 my wife and I had our house renovated and the contractor took our money but didn't complete the job. I started taking a lot of unpaid time off work trying to finish the renovations and we were getting badly into debt. I had my third Traffic Sergeant who didn't like me much and I didn't like him either. He was thought to be a back stabber by most of the guys on the police department. Most of the 'Old Guard' in the Traffic Division as we were named by the bosses had been transferred and my Sergeant Frank Baldwin or Frank the knife as the patrol members called him, thought it was time for me to go. He was right; I went back to Patrol. Frank would tell people that I had an attitude problem but in keeping with Franks' reputation he would never say that to my face, just behind my back.

Back To the Doldrums

December 1983 I have been transferred back to Patrol South, Team 6 working out of the Oakridge sub station again. Team 6 included the Mount Pleasant area which had a fair number of welfare and drug types in the vicinity. When I was in Traffic I was getting cold riding the bike in the winter and knew it was time to go, but all the old traffic players had been split up and it's like being on the job again for the first time. Tom Ridgewell and Al Hutton from Traffic were about the only guys on my new team I really knew.

While in Traffic I hadn't realized our reputation was so bad until I came back to Patrol. The first day back I am assigned to work with Paul Ballard who may have been on the job for 2 years. As we are walking in the Oakridge parking lot towards our parked police car, we introduce ourselves. Paul says" Oh, you're Doug Barker. Your name was mentioned at the police Academy as one of the members from Traffic that were shit disturbers". His Academy instructor, Bob Murrey, had said this to the class. It was amazing as Bob Murrey and I didn't know each other at the time but he would have picked this up from other disgruntled supervisors.

My being back in Patrol meant back to a midnight shift that I hated. I am depressed at work and not having much fun. My wife and I are struggling with financial problems because of having to use all our credit cards to get the house renovations completed. Things were pretty tight financially right now and of course it didn't help that I'm on my third marriage and left a lot behind with the other two wives. When I'm at work I would get a call to some scum bag's place that is on welfare and see they have better things than my wife and I have and we are both working. Of course the other guy's stuff is probably stolen.

* * *

In Patrol you are either a one man car or teamed up with a partner. A partnership is like a marriage; it can be very good or horrible. You are with this person 10 hours a day supposedly sharing the work load and you get to know each other pretty well. My Sergeant teams me up with John Hossack who is senior to me on the job and seems to have his own issues. I figure I'm back in patrol and I will try and make the best of it but this partnership isn't working. John and I are on different wave lengths. We both know the boss is watching us like a hawk and John suggests we try and get the most squad arrests for the month. We do pretty well for the month and get something like 25 arrests. That's it though, John loses interest after that.

One Friday night John and I are working together and it is a busy night. We are assigned to a break- in of a low end clothing store on East Broadway. When we arrive at the store the front window has been kicked in and the place is pretty much cleaned out. We have to keep the premises secure and wait for the store's reference to arrive to determine what was taken and arrange for the premises to be boarded up. This will take some time, maybe hours. In the meantime it's getting crazy out there and other police units near by are calling for help. John and I leave the insecure premise to assist the other units calling for help. Of course the Department procedure is not to leave an insecure premise but it is difficult to listen to the calls for assistance and not do anything.

A short time later Inspector Dave Athens calls us on the police radio to return to the insecure store. He goes up one side of us and down the other and ends up writing a complaint. It seemed to us the store was the least important priority when someone was calling for help and we were so close. Inspector Athen's letter of complaint didn't bother me terribly because I could see his point but it was a fast decision we made. I got to know Dave Athens better later on in my career and we still disagreed on the decision.

John was always taking time off of work or taking the last 4 hours off of the afternoon shift to go to the Police Club. I would arrive at work and see his car in the parking lot with his Martin Mull Leisure Suit hanging in his car and I knew I was going to be working alone again for the last 4 hours of the shift. This happened all the time and I finally requested a new partner.

* * *

Policemen like everyone else have good days and bad days; times when you're not feeling 100% or you're just in a bad mood for some reason. If you're in a job that isn't dealing with the public being in a bad mood may not be significant, but if you're in the service industry it might not be a good thing. I volunteered to be the Police Wagon driver one night as the regular person booked off sick. I was in a grumpy mood for some reason and driving the wagon and picking up prisoners was a fairly easy job as it didn't require any reports. All you had to do was pick up the prisoner from the arresting officer and drive the prisoner to the Police Station and hand him over to the Jail Guards. I pick up this guy who had been arrested for being drunk by some patrol members near Nanaimo and Kingsway and I start driving towards the jail. The guy is a real mouthpiece and he's spitting on the glass between the back of the wagon and the drivers compartment. The guy is yelling and swearing and then he starts mooning me with his bare ass through the glass partition and I decide I've had enough. I start hitting the gas and then the brake and the gas and then the brake. My prisoner starts flying around the back of the wagon. I thought that would do it but it didn't, he kept it up. I was so pissed off when I got to the back of the station I opened the wagon door to escort him to the jail and I popped him one right in the kisser. I realized I had lost my cool and went to the Station NCO and told him about it and I booked off sick before anything else happened that night.

* * *

I am working a one man day shift car and it's getting close to going home time. Its pouring rain and I pull over an old car that had gone through a stop sign near Trout Lake. The car comes to a stop and I radio my position to the operator. The car then starts to slowly back up and hit my patrol car. I run up to the drivers door and open it and put the car in park and turn off the ignition. The driver is an older male about 70 years old and he seems pretty inebriated. When I opened the car door it smelled like a bloody bakery. I look on the floor behind the driver's seat and there are 14 empty bottles of Vanilla Extract used for cooking. I wish I had never seen this guy because it is time to go home and I'm tired but I call for a police wagon and I take the guy downtown for a Breathalyzer Test. The BTA operator gives him the test and the guy blows .40 when the legal limit is .08. Most people would be dead with a reading like that but this old guy was obviously an alcoholic and probably functioned every day with a high reading.

* * *

On December 10, 1984 I am working the afternoon shift with Tom Ridgewell and it has tried to snow but then changed to sleet. While in Patrol I have not been given regular police oxford shoes that they wore at that time, so I am still wearing my high motorcycle boots with my patrol uniform pants pulled over them. The shift is over and Tom and I return to the police parking lot at the Oakridge sub station. I have been driving and I get out of the vehicle and go to the back door to get my brief case out of the car. I slip on the ice, fly into the air and crash down on my left leg hurting my left knee, the same knee I injured playing rugby. I fill out the WCB forms, change into my civilian clothes and drive myself to the UBC Hospital. Life will never be the same. I am off work for several weeks and then I try returning. The knee is still giving me pain and I can't run very well. I go off work again for several weeks and then give it another try. In July 1985 the Workers Compensation Board denies my claim stating the problem is from my rugby injury and not the slip in the parking lot.

Unfortunately I will never be the same physically and in another 14 years I will discover that WCB was not truthful with me about my injury.

* * *

I have reached the point that so many Police Officers get to, the 7 to 10 year itch, where you ask yourself, is this what I want to do the rest of my life? I am concerned that I may not be very effective because of the pain in my knee and the limited running ability. I am not the physical specimen that I was in 1975 when I joined the job. I come up with an advertising brain wave where I will sell advertising on plastic bags and have them distributed through the hundreds of corner grocery stores throughout the Lower Mainland. I get myself assigned to work steady afternoon shift in the radio room and during the day time I am trying to promote my advertising business. I have every mom and pop corner grocery store in the Lower Mainland signed to a contract that they will use my bags and now I have to sell to the advertisers. It was a great idea at the time with Expo coming the next year and I had some very interested customers but I couldn't close the deal. With both jobs I was working 14 hours a day for months and no results. It was a great learning process but it didn't put food on the table. One day a friend at work said if I put as much effort into my police career as I did in the bag business I would get promoted. I knew he was right.

* * *

My knee is still giving me problems so the Department temporarily assigns me to assist in a newly formed B&E Task Force which is more Detective follow up work and not as physically demanding. My old Traffic buddy and recent partner Tom Ridgeway was recently transferred to this unit as well on a temporary basis. One day I get a call from our Identification Unit that they have got a positive finger print from a B&E that occurred some time ago and the owner of that print is Shawn McNeil who is presently doing time in Oakalla Prison, two years less a day, for other B&E's that he has committed. I call the prison and make arrangements to go and interview him. Tom isn't working this day so I go alone. The prison guard leads me to an interview room and then they bring in Shawn from the cells. Oakalla prison is a medium security prison and just like those prisons you see in the movies with the several tiers of open cells. Oakalla is about to be closed very soon and moved out to Abbotsford under a new name. I tell Shawn that I am investigating a B&E where his finger prints were found. I also tell him because he is already doing time, if he cooperates we could clear this case as him being responsible with no extra jail time and get the case off our books as being solved. He warms up to this and admits breaking into this particular house on the west side of Vancouver and most important he tells me what he took when he broke into the house. I make notes of this and tell Shawn I will have to check out his story and I will get back to him but it might be a good idea if he tells me about any other B&E's he's done. I tell him it would be a shame for him to be released from Oakalla in about 6 months only for us to find more of his finger prints at a previous B&E and then he goes back to prison. Shawn thinks about this and tells me he can show me a lot more places if I can get him out of Oakalla for the day so he could point out his victim's houses. I tell him I will get back to him.

I check out Shawn's story with the original B&E report and it all matches to what he said. The next Saturday Tom Ridgeway and I go to Oakalla and with lots of paperwork and our careers on the line, have Shawn released to our custody for the day We hit the west side of Vancouver and Shawn would say drive here, turn there and point out a house and say he broke into it. He would have a rough idea when it was, daytime, nighttime, time of year but not the exact date. We would make notes of the items he said he took to the best of his recollection and anything unusual. We took Shawn for a hamburger and about 6 hours later returned him to the Oakalla prison. The next week Tom and I have to go to Headquarters and try and find the reports to match all these cases Shawn has given us. We find the reports and end up clearing 21 B&E files. One file the victim reported a mountain bike, a TV, a VCR, some alcohol and a silver tea service as being stolen when in fact Shawn said he only took the bike and some booze. We showed Shawn the report later and he stuck to his story that he only took the bike and the booze. While it appeared the victim was doing an insurance fraud, it was a thief's story against a tax payer's but we believed Shawn.

* * *

I am approached one day by an Inspector and asked if I would be interested in doing crime prevention work and I agree. I get assigned to do crime prevention for all of the District 3 Patrol area. It is a bit of a suck job, not very exciting, but it is steady days with weekends off. Because of this position I am around the bosses more and they seem to like what I am doing in the community. I am working hard and trying to be creative in some new crime prevention methods and not just putting in time. I am beginning to see opportunities and I look at charting a course to promotion.

I have given a crime prevention lecture to a community group one evening and returned to the office to prepare to go home and change out of my uniform. I didn't work for any specific Team Sergeant but I worked directly for the Staff Sergeant in charge of the whole of District 3 and he was not around. This particular evening I had an occasion to be looking for an overtime slip in his desk and saw a folder with my name on it. Of course, being curious I open it. Inside is a letter written by my previous Staff Sergeant Ray Canuel addressed to A/Supt Laughy in charge of Staff Development. The letter is dated October 27, 1983 a month before I am transferred from the Traffic Division.

The letter says "As per your request I spoke to Sgt. Baldwin, Barker's NCO. He states that Barker is a high traffic enforcer however he has an attitude problem and according to Sgt. Baldwin a drinking problem. Further Barker has problems dealing with the public.
Sgt. Baldwin also informed me that Balm is getting the boot out of Traffic and going to Team 7. Baldwin recommended that Barker, Balm and Al Turner who are the best of friends, should not be assigned to the same squads. If they are it is his opinion that they will give their NCO's nothing but problems."

The letter closes with "It would appear that Barker has not changed since he worked for me in Team 31. He should not go to any other Team but 6. I'm sure we can deal with him."

I was shocked at finding this old report and immediately hit the photo copy machine. I knew the reputation of the 'old guard' and that backstabbing Frank hated me as much as I and everyone else hated him, but I didn't think anyone would have this information lying around in print.

The next day I drove down to Headquarters and saw Ray Canuel who had now been promoted to Inspector. I walked into his office and he greeted me warmly and asked what he could do for me? I closed the door to his office and explained that I had been in his old desk at the Oakridge sub station and found this letter and handed it to him. Then I sat down and watched him read the letter. As he read, he appeared somewhat sheepish. I told Ray I wasn't very happy that this letter was on my file and it was over 2 years old and still sitting in that desk. I asked him how many people may have seen that letter over the past two years. I also said if Sergeant Baldwin felt that way, why had he not come and talked to me in person about my attitude and perceived drinking problem. I asked "Isn't that what a good boss or NCO should do, talk to the employee about his or her problem?" Backstabbing Frank Baldwin knew I had problems with my house and that I had 12 liens on it after the contractor ran off with our money but he never mentioned that to Ray Canuel. Ray Canuel actually apologized for the letter still being around and said he would have the file and letter destroyed. I guess Sergeant Baldwin was the back stabber everyone said he was. There you go common sense and a lack of courage.

* * *

In order to get promoted with only 10 years service you have to be known, be a star if you're in Patrol or be promoted from a small specialty unit. Well I guess I was known but unfortunately not in a good way and it will take years to erase the damage that I had done while in Traffic. I figure the best chance for promotion because of my seniority, would be a small unit like Community Relations or Planning and Research.

A position comes available in Community Relations and the candidates are required to make a 20 minute presentation using flip charts and using an overhead projector. I arrive to make my presentation to the panel of three people and the Inspector in charge of Community Relations. At the head of the table is none other than Inspector Dave Athens, who had reprimanded John Hossack and me a year earlier for leaving the scene of the insecure clothing store. I didn't get the Community Relations job. There went my idea of a fast promotion. Inspector Athens called me to his office a few weeks later to debrief my presentation and where I could improve. Once again he and I discussed the insecure clothing store and we both agreed to disagree on the handling of the situation.

* * *

While I didn't get the job for Community Relations, the Department decided to send me on a course in Ottawa at the Canadian Police College. The two week course, Instructional Techniques, is a very difficult and well respected course for instructors. As it turns out anyone who gets a position in Community Relations or becomes an instructor at the Police Academy is required to take this course. I get on the plane for Ottawa and Steve Pranzl is on board heading to Ottawa to take the same course. Steve is the successful candidate that got the Community Relations position that I applied for. While I knew Steve briefly from my patrol team we developed a pretty good relationship while on the course.

The course was tough but a great experience   Students worked every night until at least midnight and were required to make a presentation everyday. It taught people how to stand up in front of a large group and make a presentation or a speech. This is something I was required to do in my Crime Prevention job as I would speak to groups in the community about protecting their homes and businesses.

* * *

I am back at my Crime Prevention job in District 3 making use of my Instructional Techniques Course. While I haven't been able to run or play sports for the past 2 years I have taken up a more stringent weightlifting program for exercise. However this strenuous work out and the years on the motorcycles in the cold and rain caused me to develop hemorrhoids that required surgery. One day while at work I got a call from Vancouver General Hospital and they said they had a bed for me and could I come in right away. My old partner from District Three, Detective Dave Dawson gave me a ride to the hospital and I went to check in. The lady at the Admitting Office asked "Are you Charles Leonard Barker and here for a lip operation?" I replied "No, I'm Douglas George and I'm here for a hemorrhoid operation and Charles Leonard is in fact my uncle." The lady said "Oh well, you're here so you can have the room."

I check into my room hoping they have understood that I am Douglas George and not Charles Leonard so that I don't wake up with a sore lip and hemorrhoids as well. A little Philippine nurse greets me and she tells me someone is going to have to shave my behind for the operation and would I prefer a male orderly or her to do it? I told her if it doesn't bother her, it doesn't bother me. I go through all the preparations for the mornings scheduled operation, the drugs, the intravenous and even in the middle of the night two beautiful nurses arrive and give me an enema. I wake up in the morning expecting the operation and I'm told the nurses union has gone on strike and they are sending me home.

Two weeks have gone by and I'm called by the hospital again to come back for the same operation. I get the very same room and the very same Philippine nurse. She tells me she is going to have to shave me again. I told her I was just there 2 weeks ago and I barely have a 5 o'clock shadow. It didn't matter, she shaved me anyway. I had the operation the next day and when they brought me back to my room the nurse asked if there was anything I wanted. I said I wouldn't mind a donut, thinking of the kind to sit on and she brings me a chicken dinner. That wasn't a good thing because when I ate it I was sicker than a dog. I tell this story because several years later when I'm in the Strike Force I repeat this story and I'm given the nickname of Grapes.

Only two weeks have gone by since the operation and the Police Department sends me back to Ottawa on a two week crime prevention course. This course was nothing like the previous ITC course in that it was much easier and we had a lot more free time. The down side was it was winter in Ottawa with lots of snow and temperatures of -10 degrees.

* * *

I am only back from Ottawa a few days when I get a call from Inspector Bob Burns from the Community Relations Section and he asks if I would come and see him the next day. The next day I meet Inspector Burns in his office and he tells me he has replaced Inspector Dave Athens who has been transferred and they have a position available for a Constable. Inspector Burns says they were going to go through another competition but Steve Pranzl, my classmate from Ottawa, had given him a glowing report on my behalf and why bother with another time consuming competition when I have taken the Ottawa Instructional Techniques course already. The Inspector asks if I am interested. Inspector Burns was a good hard nose guy; no bullshit or airy fairy stuff about him. He said his mind. After I said I was interested he then pointed out some things he had heard about me, but he heard I had changed and he was prepared to take me on. It's a done deal. I am transferred in a week.

Upwardly Mobile

The Community Relations Section was a small unit consisting of an Inspector, a Sergeant, a Corporal and four Constables. I was assigned to be the Crime Prevention officer and would oversee or assist other Crime Prevention Officers located throughout the city. One member was assigned to be the Business Liaison Officer, the Corporal was in charge of the School Liaison Officers that worked directly out of the schools and one member was assigned to be the new Media Relations Officer. Jim Meeker somehow worked himself into being the police Department's first ever full time Media Relations Officer. Jim fit right in; everyone that worked there was a pretty boy. The guys at that time were all handsome and looked like models and they all knew that as well. There was no place for a mutt like me. Hell, I liked to drink and smoke and swear. I was going to have to work on this. Jim did a great job as the Media Relations Officer but then it started getting to his head. He would be on TV or the radio all the time and he later told me he thought he should have his own dressing room. I burst out laughing. As it turns out years later I thought everyone that followed Jim as the Media Relations Officer seemed to forget they were originally hired as a police officer and this is just a temporary assignment. It was and still is a tough assignment as you have to think on your feet with cameras rolling and you're always on call. You end up becoming a media celebrity and you start believing your press clippings.

It didn't take long to realize how good this position could be for promotion if I worked hard. The Community Relations office was on the top floor where all the top officers of the Department are located. Not only was the office on the top floor, it was an open area right by the elevators to the underground parking lot. The Chief, all the Deputy Chiefs and Superintendants as well as all the high flying Inspectors looking for room to advance had to walk by our open area and see us at our desks. Steve Pranzl and I both lived in Richmond and car pooled much of the time. The traffic could be ugly from downtown Vancouver to Richmond so you either left early or stayed late. We stayed late. Everyday the Chief Constable, the Deputy's and Superintendants would see our open offices in the morning when they arrived and in the evening on their way home and see us at our desks. They knew your name and sometimes they would stop to talk to you. My reputation as a problem and shit disturber was beginning to fade as they got to know me better.

* * *

I had been in the position a couple of months and was getting settled in and feeling comfortable. One day my old partner Larry Young comes by the office all happy. He was getting promoted from Detective to Sergeant in a few days and he wanted to see if we had any newspaper clippings of an ERT incident from the week earlier. There had been a hostage taking incident where an estranged father was holding his small baby hostage. Anyway in the newspaper article it shows a picture of Larry in his ERT garb running and grabbing the child from the father. I told Larry I would try and find a copy for him.

The next week it is early in the morning and I'm in the bathroom at home shaving and getting ready for work. I am listening to the morning radio news and hear that last night Sergeant Larry Young was shot and killed during a drug raid. Larry had been the first ERT member through the door of a drug house in the Kitsalano neighborhood and it turned out the suspect was barricaded in his room with a rifle. I couldn't believe it. This was my old partner and my friend. A lot of tears were shed by me and all of Larry's friends and loved ones. I arrived at work still shaken up and the boss offered to let me go home but I stayed. Community Relations had a lot to do with a huge civic funeral to come and we would be busy preparing for that.

* * *

My wife and I are going over to my parents one evening and we are driving west on Park Drive and approaching Granville Street. As I attempt to merge onto Granville a small car with two males in it comes speeding north in the curb lane at about 100 km/h almost hitting us. I may have been the inventor of road rage because I went after these guys as if I was on duty. My wife is getting scared as we are in pursuit of this car and she asks what the hell I am doing. The car pulls into a driveway on Granville just south of 16th Avenue and I pull over and grab the driver as he is getting out of the car. I flash my badge and give him hell for driving like a maniac and he is very apologetic. I begin to wonder myself what the hell I'm doing. I don't have a ticket book to give him a speeding ticket and all I have done is vented my anger. I think it's the feeling of responsibility believing that everyone knows I'm a cop and I should be doing something about it. I told the guy I'm giving him a warning and returned to my car and drove off glad that the two guys were reasonable and not jerks or I could have been in trouble with my wife acting as backup. I should have remembered the 95% common sense and 5% smarts rule.

* * *

One of my assignments as the Community Relations Crime Prevention Officer is to be in charge of a police display at the up and coming Home Show at BC Place. Inspector Burns tells me I am to get the police department invited to participate in the show but with no expenses. The Home Show of course is where building suppliers, contractors etc show off their wares and they pay a lot of money to have a booth. Inspector Burns says I am to get it for free. I am given an assistant, Shelly Dwyer who is a Reserve Police Officer and she will assist me in coordinating other Reserve Officers to man the Home Show display. I am not looking forward to this project but the Reserves are pretty gung ho and have done it before.

The evening before the show begins I commandeer two police paddy wagons to move our Crime Prevention display to BC Place. We get our vehicles into the domed building and then I search out the shows organizer to see where we are to set up. The organizer tells me our booth will be located under some stair well where we will never be seen and the Reserves are furious. They have done this Home Show before and advise me it isn't worth being at the show if we are stuck there. In fact they may have trouble getting volunteers to help. While I wasn't excited about doing the Home Show I knew it was important to Inspector Burns and I didn't want to mess this project up. I decide I better phone Bob Burns at home.

This is the spring of 1987 and there aren't many cell phones around yet, at least I don't have one. I find a phone booth inside the building but I only have a quarter for change on me. Inspector Burns lives in the suburbs which is a long distance phone call. I make a blunder and call collect. Inspector Burns teenage son answers the phone and the operator advises the boy that she has a collect call from Doug Barker for Inspector Bob Burns and will they accept the call? The son yells to his dad that there is a collect phone call from a Doug Barker and I can hear some talking in the background. The son returns to the phone and tells the operator he's sorry, they won't accept the call and hung up. I was dumbfounded. How embarrassing is this? What do I say to the Reserves who are helping me? How do I face Inspector Burns in the morning when I show up for work? Luckily we were able to get a better booth and we moved in. We returned the vehicles to the police station and I took Shelly and the other volunteers to the Police Club for a drink and relayed my story about the phone call.

The next morning after a sleepless night of fuming, I arrive at work and I'm sitting at my desk. Inspector Burns is always early in the office and I try and avoid him this morning. I am not going to give him the satisfaction of my going into his office to discuss the matter. I wish I had. He comes out of his office into the open area smiling and in a loud voice and in front of everyone says, "OK Doug, what was so important to call me collect last night?" Everyone started laughing and I felt pretty small. I must have turned several shades of red and I was getting pissed off. I said to him it doesn't matter because he didn't take the call. Then I said for all he knew I was calling to say the Chief had died, but he would never have known. I was the brunt of the joke for some time to come. Bob Burns never held a grudge and would accept the criticism but I think he still has the first dollar he ever made. I was pretty mad at the time but I laugh about it now.

* * *

The first level of promotion is to the Corporal/Detective rank. About 6 years earlier you were either promoted to Detective or Corporal but the Department found more people wanting to be Detectives than supervisors so the rank became interchangeable. It worked to the Department's advantage but there were definitely people who were better in one position than the other.

I have been busy studying, writing the promotional exam and then going through the assessment centre where there is role playing as if you were a supervisor. Each year all the sections of the Police Department, Patrol, Traffic, Community Relations etc. put forward their qualified candidates for promotion. Each section places their candidates in a numerical order which is worth so many points. It is a long and stressful process and I am placed as the number one candidate out of Community Relations. I felt great that my hard work was paying off. Unfortunately there were hard feelings from one of my work mates, Teri Keller who was junior to me on the job but senior to me in Community Relations. Teri was a matronly type of policewoman who never got her hands dirty out on the streets but did a very good job in Community Relations and she was well liked by everyone including me. She was mad because I was rated higher than her from our section for the promotion and she felt I had taken her rightful spot. I think Teri was also mad because of my past reputation as a trouble maker and that I'm now rated higher than her when she was squeaky clean. Welcome to the real world. It often occurred in the Department and perhaps in the private sector that you might solve your problem if you promote your problem and get them on your team. She barely spoke to me ever again and it became awkward in the office. If Teri answered a phone call that was intended for me, instead of telling me I'm wanted on the phone she would tell someone else so they could say the phone call was for me. I think our Sergeant was getting a little annoyed at her immature behavior. She got promoted anyway the next year but we never spoke again.

At the end of the lengthy process I am told I will be promoted within several months. I think I came third out of seven candidates who were promoted but the actual promotion was by seniority so I had to wait my turn for a position.

* * *

It's February 25, 1988 and my wife and I are watching the Winter Olympics that are being held in Calgary. Around 10:30 pm the phone rings and my wife says it's my cousin on the phone. I take the phone and I'm told there has been an accident in North Vancouver and my Dad has been killed. I leave the house and drive to Vancouver to be with my Mom. When I get to my Moms apartment in Kerrisdale there are my Aunt and Uncle, my cousin and his wife and I am told the story. My Dad had been sick for the last couple of years and was getting quite frail. He had a pacemaker put in followed by a brain tumor requiring radiation, in general he obviously wasn't very well.

My Aunt and Uncle lived in the same apartment building as my parents and they had all been life long friends. Except for a short period they always lived within a few blocks of each other, they went on holidays together, played cards together and even belonged to the same bowling league. My Uncle Charlie (the one that was to have the lip operation) and my Dad were brothers from a family of nine kids. Charlie's wife Marj and my Mom were the best of friends in school before any of them got married. This particular night Uncle Charlie age 77 was driving with my Dad age 75 to their friend's house in North Vancouver to play poker. The house was high up on Skyline Drive nearing the bottom of Grouse Mountain and the house they were going to had a very steep driveway. Charlie drives up to the top of the driveway to let Dad out so he wouldn't have to walk up the steep incline. My Dad gets out of the car and being the gentleman he always was in life, goes towards the back of the car to help Charlie back down the steep driveway. Charlie didn't see Dad and ran over him killing him. Uncle Charlie was devastated and so was I.

Even though my Dad had been sick and it wasn't a surprise for him to pass on, this was a shock and I was having a hard time dealing with it. I was responsible for making the funeral arrangements but I needed the help of Steve Pranzl to get me through it. I had been to many sudden death calls and even required to notify the next of kin of the passing of a loved one. While it was always difficult, you could do it. It's one thing to be that strong and tough policeman when you're dealing with other peoples tragedies but it's still difficult dealing with your own.

My Dad and I were good friends and I miss him a lot. When we had the funeral service, among all our family and friends were many of my Police friends including Inspector Bob Burns and I appreciated him coming.

* * *

In May of 1988 I get promoted to the rank of Corporal/Detective and I continue to remain in the Community Relations Section. I continue with Crime Prevention only now I am overseeing other Crime Prevention Officers around the city.

I received a phone call one day from one of the investigators of the Film Classification Board and he asked if the police Department needed any video tapes. I went to the Classification Board at 8th and Main Street and met with the investigator. What they had were a bunch, maybe 50 to 60, confiscated VHS video tapes that they had seized from various places containing pornographic material. The Film Classification investigator assured me that all the tapes had been demagnetized removing whatever had been recorded. I told the investigator that I thought I could use them but I would get back to him.

I had a plan for the tapes and ran the idea by Steve Pranzl who was the acting Sergeant at the time and Inspector Burns. My plan was to use several of the Crime Prevention movies that we had made and copy them onto the newly acquired VHS tapes from the Film Classification Board. We would then distribute the tapes to the libraries throughout the city where concerned citizens could borrow the movie for their crime prevention information. Everybody agreed that it was a good idea and I picked up the boxes of tapes the next day.

The demagnetized VHS tapes are sitting in a box on the Community Relations floor and I am on the phone when Detective Gord Pyke from Internal Investigation walks by and asks if we have any spare video tapes as he needs to tape an interview of some suspect. Jim Meeker hands Gord one of my tapes from the Classification Board and Gord returns to his office. About half an hour later I'm on the phone again and Gord Pyke returns and is speaking to Jim again. Jim starts laughing and goes running into Inspector Burn's office. No sooner do I get off the phone when I hear the Inspector bellowing loudly from his office "Corporal Barker get your ass in here". As I'm walking into Inspector Burn's office Jim Meeker is walking out of the Inspector's office in stitches laughing.

Bob Burns is going ape shit. "You take those damn tapes back to the Classification Board now", he says. It turns out Gord Pyke was preparing the tape for his interview and while most of the tape was demagnetized, there was a portion that wasn't and there in plain view is some guy performing oral sex on another guy. I returned the tapes that day. The Film Classification investigator offered to run the tapes through the demagnetizer again but I said that wouldn't be necessary. It was a good plan. We all had a good laugh after the smoke had cleared.

* * *

A month or so later Inspector Burns gets transferred to another unit and we have a nice going away party for him including all the spouses at Stanley Park. He got some nice gifts and I gave him a card with a 25 cent coin scotch taped to it. On the card I wrote, this is in case you ever have to phone me. He got a good laugh out of it. He was a good guy from the old school. Once he gave you shit, that was it. It was over. So many other bosses hold a grudge and have long memories. Sometimes those other bosses forget that the rest of us have long memories as well and we remember some of their escapades as Constables before they became upwardly mobile and turned over a new leaf. I guess, just like I appeared to turn over a new leaf.

While Jim Meeker was the Media Relations Officer, everyone in the office had to be able to deal with the media. There were many occasions when Jim wasn't around or he was away on holidays and one of us would have to do the daily morning media conference at the police station or even get called out in the middle of the night and be interviewed on camera at a crime scene. In view of this, our new Inspector, Al Grandia from the grocery store robbery incident, sends Jean Dennis, a new member to the unit and I back to Ottawa for the 10 day Media Relations course.

* * *

I enjoyed going back to Ottawa on courses. I had heard this course was not difficult and actually a lot of fun where you are under the television lights and doing a lot of role playing. I always have been a ham trying to get attention. The course was great in that it taught you how to be cautious of the media and that everything is 'on the record' and just because the TV lights have shut down, doesn't mean they have stopped filming.

I am flying back east alone on a Sunday for the Monday class. Jean, or as I called her, Olive Oil because of her slender figure, was already in Ottawa visiting friends. I catch a 9 am flight direct to Ottawa but by the time I actually land, take a taxi to the Canadian Police College and check in, it's 8pm and the dining room is closed. This is the usual practice and you end up ordering a pizza in. When I check in I am given a room number in the old building and I'm told I have a roommate from a small town in Nova Scotia. I'm not crazy about this because it's unusual to have a roommate there. Anyway it's about 5pm Vancouver time and I'm hungry and could use a beer. The College has a really nice bar with cheap drinks. I drop my things off in my room and the other guy hasn't checked in yet so I pick the bed I want and leave my suit case without even unpacking and head for the bar. I end up meeting a couple of guys in the bar who are well into the sauce and discover one is from Winnipeg and one is a Superintendant from Toronto and they are both in my class tomorrow.

We close the bar down around 1am, remember its 10 pm in Vancouver, and go to our respective rooms. I open the door to my room and I see my roommate has arrived and is asleep on his bed. On the night table beside his bed is a Bible and a bunch of religious magazines. Right away I know this isn't going to work out. Instead of unpacking I quietly slip out the door and go back and see the Commissionaire at the front desk. I tell him the story and add I am a terrible snorer and this isn't going to work out. He tells me there are no other rooms available and I'm stuck with it.

It wasn't good. The only good thing was it was just a ten day course and my room mate went to visit someone for the weekend so I only had to deal with him for seven days. I saddled myself up with the guys from Winnipeg and Toronto and went to bed late every night when my roommate was asleep. When the course was over and I was back home my Nova Scotia roommate sent me a card hoping I would see the error in my ways and that he would pray for me and my sins. I thought that was nice of him but I didn't write back and say so.

* * *

I am attending a two day Crime Prevention Seminar at the Richmond Hyatt Hotel where there are Crime Prevention Officers from Police Forces all around the province as well as civilian volunteers. There are probably several hundred people attending with Dignitaries such as the British Columbia Solicitor General and even Chief Constable Bob Stewart from the Vancouver Police. I had a female Reserve Constable who shall remain nameless, assist me at the conference which was followed by a very nice dinner. A lot of Mounties were doing their best at putting on the moves on this attractive assistant of mine and I decided it was time for me to go home. The assistant had booked a room for herself at the hotel which was a good thing I discovered the next day.

I return to the hotel the next morning as there is a breakfast meeting and the Dignitaries are going to make some speeches. I am sitting beside my assistant who is looking terrible and I realize this person had too much to drink last night. We are seated at round tables with eight to a table and our table is right at the front by the podium. Vancouver's Chief Bob Stewart is making his speech and I see my assistant reach into her purse and remove what appears to be a plastic sandwich bag. She then slowly bends forward with her head under the table and ever so quietly throws up into the plastic bag. I could see the bag filling up and I hoped it would stop soon before it overflowed. There was no Stomach wrenching or the head throwing back like I would be doing, just a very quiet fill up. I don't think anyone else at our table knew what was happening or even Bob Stewart. I felt terrible for her and how embarrassed she must have been but, I thought she was pretty classy in the way she handled the situation.
Shortly after this incident, January 1989 I am transferred to the Vancouver Strike Force as a Detective.

Graduation Day with My Mother – May 1976

Kat's Rugby Game – all eyes focused on the ball

Results of being kicked in the head in a Police Rugby Game - I had to work like this for 2 weeks

Motorcycle Drill Team West Van Parade colliding with Don MacLaron and Dave Clarke - June 6, 1981

Being lifted off the bike by Lou Williams as civilians and West Vancouver Police hold the motorcycle – note the crash bar snapped off

Courtesy of the North Shore News

Getting ready for Drill Team Practice – 1982

Inspection - Queen Elizabeth and Prince Phillip leaving Vancouver
- March 1983 – I'm second from the right
Courtesy of the Vancouver Sun Newspaper

Quiet time in the Strike Force

Typical Drug Squad Disguise

Living on the Edge

The Vancouver Strike Force is a highly trained surveillance unit
that also has the capability of making arrests of dangerous
offenders when need be. The unit was formed around 1985 and
was intended to work on short term projects of no longer than 2
weeks in order to assist the various Divisions in the Department
such as Patrol and Major Crime. The unit uses leased vehicles,
some are high end cars, and the unit is well armed for dangerous
takedowns. In 1989 when I am assigned to the unit there are two
ten man squads with each squad comprised of a Sergeant, one or
two Detectives and the remainder of the team being Constables.
All the members, no matter what rank, will serve for two years and
then be transferred. The stress level is high and the hours so long
that when the two years are up, even though you have loved the
work, most people are ready to move on to a different assignment.
The turnover is gradual with a member leaving every 4 or 5
months and a new replacement coming in. It takes a good six
months to learn the job and mistakes are subject to high criticism
in order to improve quickly. Every day the squad debriefs the
surveillance so that mistakes are addressed and we discuss what
can be done to improve our techniques. You have to learn quickly
because no sooner do you become an expert and it's time for you
to be transferred. You either have a knack for surveillance and
role playing or you don't. There have been many excellent police
officers go into the Strike Force only to get kicked out because

they couldn't stand the boredom or the pressure at the moments of terror. There are times you have to forget you're a policeman and play the role of a scumbag and some people can't do that. The reputation of the Vancouver Strike Force at the time and perhaps to this day, was purported to be the best surveillance unit around. The RCMP have their own unit, Special O, which may be as good but they do not get involved in arrests or takedowns to the extent of the Strike Force.

* * *

Before I can join my squad I am required to take the Vancouver STAR Course, (Surveillance Techniques and Resources) Doing proper surveillance can be very difficult and it's nothing like you see on television where some cop has followed the bad guy for miles all by himself and the bad guy doesn't know he's there. Good surveillance is teamwork and you are as good as your weakest link. The road boss is in charge of the squad when doing surveillance. He is like a quarterback in football. He calls the plays and assigns people to various positions and duties, all on the fly when we may be doing 100 kilometers per hour or the crooks are just leaving the bank. He is keeping track of where everyone is, talking on the cell phone and trying to make the right decision sometimes while we are on the move. When the surveillance starts and we get moving, the car behind the suspect has control and he is called the eye. The vehicle behind the eye and ready to take over the eye is called the back door and then there are parallel cars should the suspect's car turn right or left. Most of the cars have a passenger that is wired for sound and he or she is called the foot. The feet do all the hard work and usually are the ones with the best view of the crime taking place. The primary task for the driver of the surveillance vehicle, while important not to get burned, is to carry the feet from one location to another. A lot of the people you work on are big time criminals and they are not all stupid. They are looking for surveillance, sometimes doing counter surveillance moves but while they see you, they don't think and don't want to believe you're a cop so they carry on.

* * *

The course has been going well and so far I haven't had to do much in the way of strenuous running to test my bad knee. We are on the last day of the course and one of the instructors advises us Major Crime has asked if we could work on a couple of bank robbers that are both known drug addicts. We are shown pictures of these two guys and one of them is known as Harvey the Newf, no doubt he is from Newfoundland. We have been following them the better part of the day and they lead us to the area of Broadway and Main Street. The eye has said one of the guys has gone into the bank and the other is keeping six, (being the lookout) outside the bank. The radios for the feet in those days could be pretty scratchy at best and I'm not getting everything over the radio. My driver gets me a block away from the bank and drops me off. I run, trot or hobble my way to Broadway and Main and I see Harvey standing in front of a bakery on the west side of Main Street. Another foot, Bernie Holman, a police woman, is inside the bank and calling everything the other guy is doing. As I was approaching the area I had come from the south and walked north on Main towards Broadway and saw the Royal Bank on the north east corner of Broadway and Main and believed this is the bank that is going to get robbed. I am so focused on Harvey; I haven't realized that there are 3 different banks at that intersection all at different corners. I hear Bernie say on the radio that the other guy has approached the teller and then Bernie gets excited and she says he has handed the teller a note. Within a minute Bernie says, "He's leaving, he's leaving" and with that the door beside me flies open and the other guy and Harvey are off and running north on Main and across Broadway. At that point I look and see just to the north of the bakery is a CIBC Bank and I follow in hot pursuit. I almost get hit by the east west Broadway traffic as I run across the street and Detective Bill Parnell is struggling with Harvey against the wall of a building trying to handcuff him and there is money falling all over the place. I am pissed off at my stupidity and I lose my temper and throw Harvey to the ground as Bill completes the handcuffing. I thought, I'm going to like this job.

* * *

The driving in the Strike Force is unbelievable. When you are the eye or the back door you are semi relaxed if the suspect is driving normally. Everyone else is driving like a mad man though as they are trying to keep up with you on parallel streets. You are speeding, running red lights and stop signs and driving on the wrong side of the road just like the movie the French Connection. It has to be done or the suspect is gone. If you are following a person who is going to rob a bank or has kidnapped someone you can't lose them. If you are the eye and the suspect runs a light you have to stop. You can't let him see you run the light or the jig is up. One of the parallel cars will pick him up or you run the light as soon as the suspect is out of sight and you try and catch up. It is done as safely as possible but the adrenalin gets running pretty high. You get a lot of unhappy people giving you the finger because they think you look like some long hair asshole and they don't realize that these same assholes are the cops.

Being a Detective in the Strike Force is not like any other Detective work other than perhaps the Drug Squad, which is a close second. You show up to work in an office at the station just to get your equipment and then you are quickly out to the site that you are working on. Other than rank, the Detective and the Sergeant are just part of the team and have to get their hands as dirty as the constables who are working for them. Surveillance is hours of boredom with short periods of sheer terror and excitement.

The moment guys get into the Strike Force they start growing their hair and beards. I think it's done for two reasons. One reason is the fact you have been clean cut and in uniform for so long (not to mention the weekly inspections) so you enjoy the change. The other reason is it builds up your self confidence in playing the role of someone other than a cop. Some guys go to extremes with their beards down to their chest and others go and get earrings. The beard was fine for me, besides I wasn't sure which ear the earring was worn on to signify if you were a mariner or if you were gay and I didn't know much about either life style.

* * *

I have been in my new squad only a few weeks when a Patrol
Constable provides the Strike Force with some information that a
video store robbery is planned to take place within the next week
and he also gives us the name of the prime suspect. According to
the constable the store is at Hastings and Lakewood and it may be
an inside job intended to collect some insurance money. The main
suspect is an East Indian male about 23 years old who has been
making a name for himself as an up and coming thug and gang
member. The guy lives in the area of Kingsway and Carolina and
we have been watching him for several nights without any action.
I am a foot and it's my turn to be the eye on the suspect's house
from the open park to the south. It's about 2 am and I see the
suspect's neighbor walking into the park from the north and he's
walking two Doberman dogs. I can't give up the eye but I don't
want this guy to see me either. I find a Jungle Jim that kids climb
and play on and I climb up to the top and lay down. The guy
unleashes the dogs as they run around the park and the two dogs
stop under the Jungle Jim. My heart is pounding. The dogs are
looking around the Jungle Jim and I have no excuse for hiding
there other than being a pervert. I am not very fond of dog bites
either. Finally the man and his dogs walk away and I calm down.
The remainder of the night is uneventful.

The next night, a Friday and the suspect leaves his house and
meets up with three other guys and they begin driving around in
this old blue van. It's about 9:30pm and we start driving east on
East Hastings Street into the community of Burnaby where the van
pulls into a gas station. We watch as one of the occupants fills up
a 5 gallon can of gasoline. The van then continues east. I am a
foot this night and riding with Marilyn McTait and she is driving a
nice two door grey Buick Regal. Also with us in the vehicle is the
Patrol Officer that provided the information who wants to see the
conclusion of his file and he is obviously dressed in plain clothes.

The blue van with the suspects has turned from heading east on
Hastings and is now going west on Georgia Street and Marilyn

decides to be a north parallel in the lane. The eye calls the vehicle north on the next side street and then says they're stopping. We don't want to exit the lane in case this is a heat check so the Patrol Constable who is in the front passenger seat gets out on foot to have a look for them and I stay in the back seat of the two door car. Marilyn backs the car up into a driveway at the back of a house and their security light comes on. A few seconds later the Patrol Constable runs up to the passenger door of our car, his eyes as large as saucers as he looks at us, he blurts out "They're coming", and then he runs away north between the houses. It is too late to just drive away so Marilyn quickly pulls on the reclining lever so she is half in the back seat and I am sitting on the right side of the back seat. She tells me to start making out with her which I was more than happy to do. There is a tapping on the passenger front window and I look up and it is one of the suspects. The guy, not the prime suspect, asks why we are following them and I tell him to fuck off, can't you see we are busy. We then go back to making out and the guy leaves and they eventually drive away.

The Patrol Constable gets back in the car with us and the surveillance leads us to the video store at Hastings and Lakewood in a strip mall that has about four stores and a Chinese restaurant. The suspects enter the front of the video store which is still open for business but we are unable to see inside. About 10 minutes later one of the suspects exits the front door and drives the van to the rear of the store and we watch as they begin unloading hundreds of video tapes from the store's back door into the van. About an hour has passed since they started loading the tapes and I am back in the car with Marilyn as someone else is holding the eye on foot as well as our Patrol Constable. We have the store surrounded and both ends of the south lane covered and we are asking Sergeant Bob Thompson who is the road boss, what he wants us to do. What is the plan? Well, he says, he would like to see where the videos go, who all is involved and so on. We are concerned we could lose them after watching the crime and then we have nothing and we say so. Then one of the suspects comes out and gets the 5 gallon gas can and goes back inside the store. Again we ask, Bob what is the plan? Bob says he is thinking about it. Then all the suspects come out and start getting into the van to drive away west in the lane. People are asking what we are doing. Things are about to happen. Bob then says ok, take down, take down. Marilyn and I drive into the lane from the west end and as we enter the lane we hear a shot and I see one of our members, Doug Lewis fall to the ground. The suspects were all arrested inside the van and there was a loaded hand gun near the driver's seat but it had not been fired. It turned out the Patrol Constable was in a back yard and when he tried to shoot out the tires of the van it ricocheted and hit Lewis in the leg. I learned a lot from this incident. You have to make a decision quickly so the other members can be prepared to do what they have to do. Sometimes it's best to take what you're given than to be greedy and risk everything to get one more player. Sergeant Bob is a smart guy but can't make a fast decision at crunch time. He always wanted everything perfect but it never works that way. The other thing I learned was shooting out the tires is more difficult than on television.

In 1989 and 1990 the Strike Force worked on all types of cases that were presented to us, any cases that were causing major problems to specific units. That was the mandate for starting the unit in the first place. We worked on professional shoplifters, the Gypsies, B&E suspects, pedophiles, rapists, bank robbers and even murder suspects. A few years later the unit seemed to be more focused on Major Crime projects and less on the smaller but just as troublesome offences.

* * *

One night around 2am we were watching a couple of bumbling B&E artists in Surrey. Yes we went everywhere in the Lower Mainland. They have taken their mini pick up truck to the back of a strip mall and attached a chain from the vehicle's bumper to the door of the building. They backed up quickly in order to pull the door off the wall but instead pulled the bumper off the truck. Our member in the eye position while trying to be quiet started to laugh as he was repeating the events over the radio. They quickly got the bumper and chain into the back of the truck and left. They did a B&E about 40 minutes later at a different location breaking the front plate glass window and we took them down in the usual aggressive Strike Force manner.

We have been watching this little Vancouver B&E group for about four days and at times we think we have been burnt and they are on to us. It's the summer time and on the Friday night the four guys pile into their car and gas up at Grandview and Rupert. You always know something is going to happen when they gas up; it always does. We follow them all the way out to Langley and they go to a Mac's Milk by the Willow brook Mall. We have several people out on foot and three of the suspects go into the store and one stays with the car. Two of the suspects keep the store proprietor busy with stupid questions and make some small purchases while the third guy who is smaller in stature climbs into the milk cooler that leads right back to the store room. Our people at the back of the store see the stores rear door open and cases of cigarettes start flying out the back while the other two suspects are still talking with the proprietor. Take down is called and these guys go running. Two guys go running towards the Willow Brook Mall parking lot and get tackled and take a bit of a thumping before being handcuffed. That was the way it was done, no head shots but a few to the body. Perhaps not much will happen in court but they will remember the arrest. Anyway, there were lots of shoppers screaming at the commotion and as we looked like thugs ourselves they thought it was some kind of a gang fight until the handcuffs came out. The next day everyone shaved off their beards in case there was some major investigation of Police brutality and the witnesses were required to identify the officers.

* * *

We worked on the Gypsies who were ruthless; the women would wear those large dresses that hang down to their ankles and they have aprons hidden underneath the dress. They have been known to steal a chainsaw from a store concealing it under their dresses. We watched a car load of Gypsy women in Surrey approach an old couple that were working in their front yard. One of the Gypsy women pretends she is sick and asks the elderly lady if she can get a glass of water. They go inside the house with the elderly wife leaving her husband outside in the yard. While the elderly lady is getting water for the sick Gypsy, the second Gypsy woman cleans out the jewelry from the victim's bedroom. The suspects then walk away saying thank you for the water. We had Dave Carlson go inside the victim's house in order to confirm they were robbed while we followed the carload of Gypsies away from the house. When Dave radioed to say that the older couple had in fact been robbed we did a tactical vehicle take down and arrested them and recovered the jewelry that was taken. They didn't like being arrested by the Strike Force either.

* * *

One thing we did work on a lot was bank robberies. We would get information from the Homicide Robbery section about a specific suspect and we would go into action. Most bank robberies would only yield about $1500 dollars and it can be a tense time for everyone, the teller and the robber, because he is really implying a threat and he hopes everything goes well. The bad side is most, not all, bank robbers are drug addicts with a heavy addiction and depending on what drug they are using they can be quite unpredictable or violent. The Bank Robber needs more money than they are going to get from doing a B&E. They get the cash right away as opposed to having to lug your stolen property to a fence and get ten cents on the dollar. They know the banks have cameras and they are taking their picture but they are that desperate they do the robbery anyway. They pull off the robbery and depending on their drug use, they are able to buy more drugs until the money runs out. Sometimes we knew the robbers drug habit ahead of time and we had a good idea when the money would run out and when they would have to do another robbery. The drug addicted robber would be doing another robbery in 4 days at a $500 a day drug habit. Occasionally you would get the robbers that were really aggressive, showing a gun and jumping the counter but most often it was one person that would quietly produce a note to one teller, get her money and calmly slip out of the bank before everyone else knew what had happened.

* * *

There was a Native Indian fellow Henry Johns who had pulled a lot of bank robberies over time and he would produce a note such as "I have a gun, give me all your money". The note is hand written and if it is left at the bank it is good evidence. For some reason this particular fellow is arrested at home by the Strike Force. He is taken away and two members stay behind and wait for the Robbery Detectives to arrive. While these members are waiting, one of the guys decides to finish the partially completed crossword puzzle that the suspect had been working on. The Detectives arrive and the two Strike Force members leave. The Robbery Detectives are elated because they see the crossword puzzle and now have some hand writing to compare against the robbery notes Henry Johns had left behind at the banks. Unfortunately the Detectives find out this Strike Force Constable had completed some of the puzzle and they had to get him to try and remember which answers were his and which answers were the suspects in order to do a handwriting comparison.

* * *

There has been a female that pulled several bank robberies and we are approached by Major Crime with a possible suspect and a copy of the Frisco Bay photo from the bank. In the photo the white female is wearing a wide head band covering some of her forehead.

 It's a sunny Friday at the beginning of October and we have set up on the suspect's apartment building around Dundas and Nanaimo Streets. The suspect, Sylvia Lempert and a male companion, both around mid 30's in age, exit the building with two Golden Retriever dogs and they get into a large station wagon with the female driving. We follow them during the course of the day and they seem like a loving couple who would occasionally stop and let the two dogs out to run. I am a foot this day and riding with Sergeant Bob Thompson when the suspects start to circle around the CIBC Bank at Grandview Highway and Renfrew Street. Bob drops me off and I go inside a restaurant on the north side of Grandview immediately across the street from the bank. The suspects have pulled into a Pizza Hut parking lot to the west of the bank and then they start slowly driving east in the lane. I can see the female get out of the driver's seat and she walks towards the back of the car and then she goes out of my vision, but the male companion moves over and gets behind the wheel. This is beginning to look good. The female comes back into my vision and she is walking north in the east parking lot from their station wagon and I see she has changed her clothes and is wearing her famous head band. I advise the rest of the squad to be heads up as she walks into the bank. The female is only inside for a moment when I see her turn around, exit the bank and walk back towards her waiting car in the lane in a normal manner. The couple drive away and go south slowly on Renfrew Street. Sergeant Bob picks me up and we are mobile in surveillance. One of our guys, Ed Lowe gets left behind and he commandeers an ambulance to give him a lift to catch up to us.

The two suspects drive to Killarney Park where they let the dogs out again to run and the lovely couple are holding hands and watching the two dogs. At this particular era in the Strike Force history we did not have proper police Motorola radios attached to the cars, but everyone including the drivers worked off of portable radios whose frequency was not as strong. We are also in an area of south Vancouver that the portable radios pick up a lot of static. Sergeant Thompson and I are parked in a little cul de sac to the east of the park by Rupert Street and can see the activity but we are probably 300 yards away. Another member to the west calls the suspects into the car and they drive west towards Elliott Street. They drive by the Bank of Nova Scotia at 49th and Elliott and then go north towards 48th Avenue. One of our feet gets out on foot to watch the bank and Bob and I drive several blocks to the east and wait.

We are not hearing anything on the radio and we keep calling but no one is answering. Then we hear Penny Mason yelling on the radio they are following the two suspects east on 48th Avenue and then north on Vivian Street. She sounds pretty excited and I ask if they robbed the bank and she says, "Yes, they robbed the bank". Sergeant Thompson advises to do a Tactical Vehicle Takedown at the first opportunity. Brad Prentice says he will cut in front of the suspects and attempt a tactical vehicle takedown at 45th Avenue and Sergeant Thompson starts to speed up as I get my gun out. Brad cuts the suspects off and stops in front of them as Bob drives our car over the curb to be near the suspect's passenger side. We hit the curb so hard the car stalled and I hit my head on the cars roof and I almost dropped my gun. Before I could even open my car door the suspects drove around Brad's stopped car and sped off east on 45th Avenue. They are going fast and being pursued by Andy Robarts, Penny Mason and Brad. Bob gets our car going and I am trying to find our portable radio that went flying somewhere inside the car when we hit the curb. We are well behind everyone and we see the suspects run a red light at 45th and Rupert followed by our undercover police cars. We had placed a Bird Dog, a homing device, on the suspect's car the night before to assist us to locate them that morning if we had to. I get on the regular Patrol channel and come on Code 4, we are in pursuit of a vehicle that was involved in a bank robbery at 49th and Elliott. With that, Andy Robarts begins to broadcast the chase and directions and I tell Bob that we should call the chase off. I say we know where they live and we have a bird on the car. Sergeant Thompson never says anything but he slows our car down and we follow the chase from many blocks away. We are still listening intently to Andy's radio broadcast as the suspects go north on Ormidale Street and over a concrete median on Kingsway, through heavy east west Kingsway traffic and then west on Vanness Avenue. It would have been a sight to see, 4 cars appearing from nowhere and driving over a large cement median, all just missing cars on a major east-west street. The people in our cars have a red flashing light that they throw on the dashboard but there are no sirens in the cars. Bob and I are just crossing Kingsway when Andy advises they are really going fast and the suspect is all over the road. Next thing we hear Andy broadcast that there has been a major accident at Vanness and Rupert Street.

Sergeant Thompson and I arrive within 30 seconds of the accident and find the suspect's station wagon against a pole on the south side of the street facing east and steam coming from the crumpled engine. Someone yelled they are running between the houses and Bob and I drive past the suspect's vehicle and stop at the lane where Bob drops me off. I start running between houses going south from Vanness and I hear over the radio that the female is in custody. I get down to the end of the next block and I hear Penny Mason say on the radio that the male suspect is standing among the gathering crowd and he is covered in white paint. Then she calmly advises he is in custody. I walk north on Rupert Street back to the scene of the accident and I see a small white pick up truck on the lawn at the south west corner of Vanness and Rupert. It turns out the driver of this vehicle was a house painter and had a bucket of white paint in the cargo area of the truck. The driver of the paint truck had been south bound on Rupert Street and he was killed when he was struck on his driver's side by the suspects speeding station wagon 1 minute and 58 seconds after I suggested we cancel the chase.

I wasn't happy about this case. Everyone in the pursuit did a great job and what they are supposed to do. I thought the chase should have been called off because of the Bird Dog attached to their car and we could pick them up later. This was a fairly major incident and our Staff Sergeant, Ken Dobbs came out to the accident scene as well as Sergeant Paul Binkley who was involved with Critical Incidents Counseling. The squad then went back to Ken Dobbs house to complete our reports. I read what Sergeant Bob Thompson had written stating he had tried to call off the chase and I completed my report covering him as if he had tried to stop it. I couldn't sleep that night and called Binkley the next day as well as Staff Sergeant Dobbs and I told them I wanted my report back because it wasn't accurate. I met Ken the next day and I handed him my new accurate report on the incident and I told Bob Thompson he better adjust his report.

No one else on the squad agreed with me that the chase should have been called off so I was the odd man out. We were all interviewed by the Major Crime Inspector and oddly enough I was the only one that didn't get a typed copy of my interview with him. In fact, the Inspector tried to convince me that the accident may have happened even if we called off the chase because the robbers were still attempting to flee the area. He may have been right.

When the case went to court for Dangerous Driving I told the prosecutor during my pre trial interview that I had an opinion about the car chase. He told me he didn't want to hear it. When we went to trial the next day I was the only one that wasn't asked by the prosecutor about the driving or could anything else have been done to prevent the accident. As it turns out the suspects never got any money from the bank because the teller said no, she wouldn't give them any money when they held her up and they ran out of the bank. The Bird Dog was never found and either fell off during the car chase or at the accident.

* * *

Its promotion season and my turn to have some effect on someone else's career. We have all good candidates on our squad to choose from but Ed Lowe and I both think Doug Lewis is the best one. Sergeant Bob disagrees with us. Sergeant Bob wasn't crazy about Lewis because Doug spoke his mind and that often was at Bob's expense. Bob thought I was caustic because I would challenge his ideas and I guess Lewis was the same thing. Doug was put forward, perhaps not as high as what Ed and I thought he should have been and he ended up getting promoted and has done very well for himself.

* * *

I am home in bed asleep when the phone rings about 1am and it is Sergeant Bob. Bob says he has been phoned at home from the robbery section and Patrol has just arrested a couple of guys that had broken into a drug store at Woodstock and Main Street and could I come to work and go into the cells with one of the suspects. I drive to work and try and prepare a cover story for my new cell mate. I get to the office and I have a cover person who will basically babysit me for the time I am in the cells.

It's pretty quiet in the jail when my cover person takes me up to the booking desk so I don't really have to put on a show for other prisoners. The jail guard knows I am a cop and walks me down the hall with rows of barred cells, hands me a 2 inch thick rubber mat for a mattress and opens the cell door. The guard sends me inside an 8 foot by 10 foot cell with an open toilet in the corner and an upper and lower bunk bed. My new roommate, the suspect, is asleep on the bottom bunk, leaving me the top one. I throw the blue mat on the top bunk and climb over my roommate onto the top bed. Back in those days prisoners were allowed to smoke in the cells if you had them and I knew my smokes would be like gold if this guy smokes, which most crooks did. The Vancouver jail is pretty old and it's just like the movies with the open bars and the guards walking by all the time.

I try lying on the bed and going to sleep but it's terribly uncomfortable so I sit up and have a smoke. I am blowing smoke all over the place hoping I can wake this guy up so we can start talking, that's what I'm there for. After about an hour the guard comes and opens the cell door and tells me I can call a lawyer and lets me out of the cell. The guard leads me to a room where my cover person is. The cover person is Marilyn McTait and she has a coffee and a sandwich for me and asks how things are going. I tell her I can't wake the guy up so I have nothing to report and I'm sent back into my cell.

The jail guard comes by about 5 am and starts serving coffee and dry toast. They don't ask if you want cream or sugar or your toast buttered. You get coffee with cream, about 4 sugars and toast with nothing on it. It's awful. I'm glad Marilyn fed me earlier. At least my roomy is waking up so I have another smoke. He asks if he can have a smoke and we are on our way. He tells me why he is there and starts to ask me about myself. I was about to tell him I had done some time back east in Toronto but just before I do he tells me he did time in Toronto. I realize this cell mate stuff isn't going to be as easy as I thought. I adjust my story to being a small time crook and only being in and out of jail in Kelowna. My roomy and I enjoy a few more smokes.

The jail guard comes and gets me and tells me I am to be finger printed and to follow him. The guard leads me back to Marilyn McTait, my cover person again in our private room. We discuss what has been happening and I tell her I need more cigarettes because I'm just about out because of my buddy. Marilyn gets more cigarettes for me and I open the pack and place the new pack in my shirt pocket. Marilyn says what are you doing? You can't do that. She continues, you can't show up with a new pack of smokes when you should only have a few left when you left the cell. She was right. That is the job of the cover person, to babysit you and take care of your needs and suggest what you might do to further your investigation. I left Marilyn the new pack but put a couple of extra smokes in the near empty pack to hold us over. My cellmate and me along with six other guys were led into a room with a two way mirror for a lineup and I thought wouldn't it be ironic if I got picked out. I wasn't picked out of course and I don't know if anything major came out of this but I learned to have a game plan and a cover story ready and pick a role that is believable.

* * *

We would work on a project and sometimes not finish it because we lose the guy or our boss calls us off to a brand new emergency. We had been working on a break and enter artist known as Murray the Mouse who specialized in apartment B&E's. We followed him to the West End near Stanley Park and he would walk the street looking for an opportunity and then buzz the intercom and enter the building. We have no idea if he is going to do a crime or if he knows someone there and our feet can't follow him into the building. About 40 minutes later he exits the building and walks nonchalantly back to his car and he doesn't appear to be carrying anything. We try and get someone into the building to see if there are any broken suite doors but it is a 12 storey building. In the mean time we are about to go mobile and we have no idea if he has done a crime or not and we aren't about to blow our cover to find out he hasn't. We let him go and we go onto another file.

Sometime later we learn Murray's MO (method of operation) is that he breaks into a place sometimes picking the lock and only takes one or two expensive items and hides them down his pants or he hides them in the buildings parking lot and comes back later to get them. This was pretty clever because many victims won't discover the jewelry theft until the next time they look in their jewelry box which may be months away and even then they may just think they misplaced it. We are assigned to Murray again and we have to devise a plan to help determine if he has committed a crime. We decide when he leaves an apartment building we will let him walk away towards his car and we will have one member on foot approach him and when they get no closer than 50 yards, say "police, I would like to talk to you". If he has stolen property on him he will probably run and we will know to take him down. If he hasn't done anything he will stop and talk to the member who can say he is an off duty officer and recognizes Murray's face as a criminal and wants to talk to him. That particular member is out of the surveillance but the surveillance unit won't be burnt.

One day we follow Murray out to the area of Nanaimo and Oxford Streets and he walks into a building. When he leaves the building we put our operation into plan and it works like a damn. He runs and we take him down and sure enough he has some jewelry and round gold balls shoved down his pants. After Murray is taken away to jail one of the members locates the apartment that was broken into. The owner is called and this 25 year old woman returns to her suite so she can tell us what was taken. She was somewhat embarrassed but told us her Benoit Balls were taken from a box that was on a mantel in the living room. None of the guys knew what these were and she was embarrassed again to explain it.

* * *

Around November 1989 there is a robbery of an armored car at the Woodwards Oakridge store. One of the Armored Guards was taking the elevator down to the main floor with all the money from the payroll department which was located on the second floor office. When the elevator door opened the guard was shot and the two robbers took off with the loot; maybe $700,000. The injured Guard lived and the culprits got away. It turns out the two suspects had robbed an Armored car in Toronto and recently in Edmonton and their names as suspects and a photo was given to the media and broadcast on the local television. The Police Department is advised by someone from a high end men's clothing store that one of the suspects had recently bought several thousand dollars worth of clothing and had not returned to pick it up. We spent about a week staking out this store in the downtown Granville Mall wearing bullet proof vests. The suspects had not returned. Then we got word that we knew where one of them was living. The robbery Detectives had already entered one of the suspect's apartments and found a filing cabinet beside the bed that contained a lot of hand guns. The Detectives removed the handguns and then proceeded to bug the inside of his apartment and then had security cameras installed in the hallway at the elevator door so we could see when he got off the elevator. Both Strike Force squads are working on this file around the clock. Our squad works the day shift and nothing happens and we do a roll over of equipment with the other squad and we go home.

I am home in bed because we will be back to relieve the other squad for dayshift when the phone rings about midnight. I am told the suspects have been arrested by the other squad and to come into the office because we are going to do a cell mate on both suspects. When I get to the office I learn that the suspect that we had been watching on dayshift came home and the other squad saw him on the security camera get off the elevator and walk into his suite. The Strike Force members then heard him open the filing cabinet drawer and then close it and then open it again. The suspect obviously saw that his guns were missing. The other squad immediately set up to take him down when he left his suite. The guy left the suite and went to the elevator where two Strike Force members with shot guns arrested him. I was told it didn't go smoothly and was touch and go for a few seconds as the suspect dropped his 357 Magnum to the floor and then reached inside his coat. The members almost opened fire but another Strike Force member appeared from the other side of the suspect and was in the line of fire. The suspect then dropped a 45 Magnum from a shoulder holster inside his coat. The suspect was wearing a bullet proof vest, had a police scanner and $10,000 in cash.
The second suspect, the partner in the robbery was arrested by the ERT unit at a different location. It turns out the two suspects had been in Winnipeg looking at committing another armed robbery and took the Greyhound bus back to Vancouver arriving that day.

Before doing the Woodwards robbery the two suspects had broken into a gun store and made off with a large quantity of hand guns. A lot of them were buried by the suspects up Cypress Bowl and weren't recovered until about a year later.

The cellmate operation went into motion. Three undercover members went in the cell with one guy and two operators went in a different cell with the other. These were much larger cells than the one I did my cellmate operation in. While it is not allowed anymore, at the time we had a member wearing a wire inside the cell. I was the cover person for one team with a recording device and the three members in the cell had a different cover person. These were two dangerous dudes. They hadn't been in the cells an hour and one of the suspects was telling the UC operators about taking the Police Nurse hostage when she came around in order to escape. The other suspect didn't like one of the UC operators because the operator had said he was in jail for drug trafficking, The suspect told the second UC operator you can't trust a drug user. I got that operator out of there. He was the same suspect that had the two guns on him when he was arrested and he told the operator he didn't know why the cops didn't shoot him when he went for his second handgun. I guess he didn't realize we had a member in the line of fire at the time. We picked up some useful information during the night and then the suspects were moved in the morning to the Remand Centre which is more secure and not the Police Department's responsibility.

We leave the jail and return to the Strike Force office. It has been a long night. I am reading a copy of the robbery report from several weeks earlier and in the report a female witness to the shooting describes the shooter as a good looking male with strawberry blonde hair. I see the robbery section has charged the first suspect with the shooting when the description fits the second suspect. I walk down stairs to the Robbery office and see Detective Ernie Reed on the phone. I wait for him to get off the phone and I just hang around. There must be a break in his phone conversation because he asks what he can do for me. I tell him I think they have charged the wrong guy with the shooting as suspect number two is a good looking guy with strawberry blonde hair and suspect number one isn't. Detective Reed says "Fuck off Barker, I know what I'm doing". I put my arms up in the air, shrug my shoulders and walked out of their office. Sometimes guys are stuck into their idea and have blinders on and won't look at anything else. When the case went to court I believe there had been an identity issue over who had actually been the shooter and a second trial was required. Both suspects were given 25 years but they could very well be out by now.

* * *

Our squad was working dayshift in August and we are back in the office getting ready to go home. Our office is right next to the Drug Squad office and the Staff Sergeant of Drugs Larry Stark asks if I would be interested in making some overtime and helping the Drug Squad out. They had a guy that wanted to sell 10,000 hits of LSD and some Hash for $10,000. I tell him I know nothing about drugs and would hardly pass for the drug type at 43 years of age. They persist and say it will be fine. Even my own Staff Sergeant, Ken Dobbs suggests I do it. I reluctantly say OK.

One of the RCMP Drug members leads me into an office where he wants the two of us to count out the $10,000 cash to make sure it is all there. This is no flash roll with a couple of hundred dollar bills wrapped around some one dollar bills or newspaper but the real thing and I had better return it. Then they tell me I am to meet a guy on the old court house stairs on Robson Street. They have given him my description so the guy will approach me. They tell me the deal won't be done there so leave the money in Christine's trunk while I'm at the meet and they will have some people watching and covering me. Christine is the nick name of the 1980 pale green four door Oldsmobile Cutlass they gave me to use. Christine is a piece of crap.

I take Christine and park her on Hornby Street and walk over to the stairs of the old court house. There are about 15 people hanging around the stairs, some at the bottom and some midway up. I have no idea what my guy looks like so I don't know if he is one of them or if he is even there yet. I try not to stare anyone down but walk to the top of the stairs to be alone. I have collar length hair and I'm wearing a red and black checkered mackinaw, a black T-shirt and blue jeans. Most of the other people on the stairs look more clean cut than I do. About 5 minutes after sitting down a guy about 23 years old approaches me and says, "Hi are you Mike?" I say I am and he says he is Clint and he sticks out his hand. I go to shake his hand and I get one of those secret squirrel handshakes with the closed fingers and then the palms and all that stuff where you need to be coordinated just to say hello. Something you used to see the brothers do on TV. Well Clint and I make small talk a bit and then he wants to know about me and where I'm from. I tell him I live in Kelowna but my old lady and I split up so I'm down in the Lower Mainland to make some money working on a fish boat. I tell Clint I don't do drugs myself but I need the money and I plan to sell the LSD at the schools when they open next month in September. He says great idea. He tells me he is giving me a good deal on this stuff and hands me a small chunk of stuff that looked like dried shit to me and I realize this is a sample of the Hash. The Drug Squad guys never told me about this part so I have no idea what I'm supposed to be doing with this brown lump of hash now that it's in my hands. I figure I guess I'm supposed to smell it so I do and say that's good stuff and hand the Hash back to Clint. I am told later I'm actually trafficking the drugs back to him when I do this. I can see a couple of Drug Squad guys hanging around the area so I feel comfortable. Clint asks if I have the $10,000 and I say I do but I have to make a stop to pick it up. He says OK but how about me coming to his place for the exchange. I don't like this idea and I say no, I would like to do a trunk to trunk exchange, both car trunks open, a fast exchange and we're out of there. I said I will meet him at the Princeton Hotel at Powell and Victoria in an hour. Clint agrees and he walks away. I wait a couple of minutes after he's left and I return to my parked car. When I get to the car I see old Christine has a right rear tire that's almost flat and I have to hurry to a gas station. I meet the drug squad members and tell them what happened and I'm going to the Princeton Hotel beer parlor to meet Clint. I tell the Drug Squad Sergeant about handing the Hash back to Clint and the Sergeant just rolls his eyes as if how stupid are you? They tell me to park Christine in an open parking lot across the street from the Princeton Hotel where they can keep an eye on the $10,000 in the trunk.

It's about 8pm and I go inside the beer parlor and sit at a table near a phone booth. I should have been off work 4 hours ago and I'm getting hungry but I order a beer and wait. This hotel is right down at the foot of Victoria by the railway tracks and the waterfront. It's a busy place in the day time with all the dock workers but it's getting quiet now and there are maybe 40 people inside with no entertainment. There has been no word from Clint and I order another beer and continue smoking my cigarettes. The phone rings behind the bar and the bartender looks at me and asks if I'm Mike. I say yes and he tells me this call is for me and I can take it at the phone booth. It's Clint and he says he's behind schedule and will be here in an hour. Things don't seem right to me. I look around the bar and don't see anyone I recognize, like a Drug Squad cover man, only a bunch of drunken goofs and I start wondering if any of them are associated to Clint. I'm realizing the Drug Squad is more concerned about their $10,000 than me. I use the pay phone and call the Drug Squad Sergeant and tell him I am tired, I'm hungry, I'm almost of out smokes and I'm getting pissed drinking beer. I tell him I don't see any cover team inside and he had better get some body in here and for them to bring me some money. About 5 minutes later one of the cover team comes inside and brings me $20 so I can get more smokes and another beer. The cover man goes and sits at a table about 30 feet away from me and we wait. About an hour later the bartender tells me I have another phone call which I take again in the phone booth. It's Clint and he's making excuses for being late and he won't be long. We go over the trunk to trunk plan again and he starts waffling about it. He says he will be here soon.

I phone the Sergeant again and tell him what's happening and that I don't feel very comfortable with Clint, something doesn't seem right. I'm feeling kind of bad that maybe I look like a wus to these guys but I don't know how long I can handle this charade and maybe I'm out of my league here. The Sergeant was pretty good about it and said for me to leave the bar, get Christine and they would meet me back at the office. I do this and I'm only in the office about 5 minutes when some of the Drug Squad members arrive and they tell me that Clint showed up just after I left with 4 other guys and they think Clint and his pals were going to rip me off for the money and all they had were the 10,000 hits of LSD, but no Hash. Clint was still arrested but I felt bad that I left too early.

* * *

Doug Lewis has done his two years in the squad and he is transferred and replaced with a new guy, Scott Hume. The squad is working some B&E types late one evening and Scott is riding with me and he's doing a good job. We follow these three guys in an old van from Vancouver out the Lougheed Highway to Maple Ridge where they start going into crime mode. With very few exceptions, these people almost point out to us what place they are going to hit. They drive around and around the area and then past the potential victim several times. The crooks often park and watch a commercial business for a while before they get up the courage to pull off the job. This particular night these guys are looking at a small drug store in a strip mall across from the Westgate Centre at 203 Street between Dewdney Trunk Road and the Lougheed Highway. Eventually these guys go into motion and take the van to the back of the store which is a one way parking lot. I am driving our nice grey two door Buick Regal and I am parked in the shadows of the Westgate Centre parking lot with a clear view of the drug store. Scotty is out of the car with an eye but he is returning to me as someone is taking his place. We know all hell is going to break loose soon and the worse part is the waiting. I start to get this twitch in my left upper leg and I can't keep it still. I'm sure it's just nerves but I want it to stop before Scotty gets back to the car. Scott gets back to me and thank God my leg has stopped flopping around like a fish out of water. We have a member at the back of the drug store keeping an eye on the three guys and the van. Two guys exit the van and wander around the front of the store carrying a garbage can and they throw the can through the front plate glass door and then climb inside the store. We are waiting for Sergeant Bob Thompson to call the takedown but he wants to wait until their van comes around the front. We wait. The guys have left the garbage can inside the front door and are taking turns filling it up with cartons of cigarettes. The eye at the rear of the store advises the van is slowly moving around the north side of the building towards the front. I quickly but quietly drive Scott and myself to the south side of the strip mall with our headlights out. The guys come running out of the drug store and Sergeant Bob yells over the radio "takedown, takedown," and we all begin to move in. I am now speeding in from the south front of the strip mall parking lot as the suspects are just getting to the back of the van. I still have no headlights on and the car becomes quieter for a second and then there is a loud thump as Scott and I hit our heads on the roof of the car. The parking lot was 2 levels, one level being about a foot higher than the other and we had been air born for a second. The van speeds off leaving the remaining two suspects behind and as the van exits the parking lot and goes south on 203 Street it hits Andy Robarts who was on foot and running to the front of the parking lot. The van is going south and the van's back door is open and swinging from side to side. Scott and I are in hot pursuit behind the van but I can hear a flop, flop, flop of a front left flat tire. I advise the guys we are losing the van and can't keep up because of the tire. Someone else takes over and they eventually get the guy in the van several miles later. I have to pull over and check for a spare tire and it's one of those skinny temporary tires. I tell Scotty he is the new man and I'm a Detective so he can change the tire. We completed our reports at the Maple Ridge RCMP Detachment and then returned to Vancouver. Scotty got even with me for the tire because he got a ride back with someone else and I drove back alone with the spare that said you should not drive faster than 60 km/h with this tire. It took me about an hour at 5 am to get back to the office and they were all gone.

* * *

Our particular squad always thought a hard take down was appropriate on these thugs who were making other peoples' lives miserable. The take down may be the most memorable part of their capture knowing that their sentence wasn't always stiff. Once the thug has been handcuffed it's over; no more rough stuff. We had a new guy on the squad who was an excellent policeman but just didn't quite fit into our type of work. He loved the rough stuff but his timing wasn't good. We arrested a guy who was a prison escapee and happened to be in a women's hair salon one day in the South Granville area. The escapee was waiting for his girlfriend as she was getting her hair done. It was day shift and we had the guy hand cuffed behind his back and we were waiting outside the salon for the police wagon to pick up the prisoner. The suspect's girl friend had given him a cigarette and it was hanging from his mouth. Our new member asked the prisoner a question and I guess he didn't like the response so he cuffed him across the face with an open hand telling him he couldn't smoke while he's talking to him. It is day light outside with a lot of people hanging about and this behavior was overboard resulting in our new member being kicked out of the squad that day.

* * *

We all had turns being made fun of by the team because we all made mistakes and some were funny. Jim Mackin was brand new on the squad and we had followed someone to the Great Canadian Super Store in Burnaby. Jim being new was naturally a foot and wired for sound. The foot can't always talk into the radio when he is out doing surveillance so we told Jim if anything unusual happens give us a heads up by double clicking the microphone on his radio. Well Jim has the suspect in the store and after a couple of minutes he double clicks his radio and we are immediately at the ready for some action. The boss asks Jim what is happening and Jim replies in a very soft voice so as to not be heard by anyone in the store that "The suspect has now moved from the Meat to the Produce Section". We all laughed and tease him to this day.

* * *

We are working a file that requires the suspect's vehicle to have a bird dog placed on it. The bird, a metal device with an antenna and batteries, has a strong magnet that is placed underneath the vehicle and it is good for about 5 days depending on the weather. These devices are expensive and we don't want to lose them. As difficult as it is putting the bird under the car, if nothing happens you have to get the bird back again and that may be more difficult than when you first put it on. Its night time and we are at 12th and Victoria and Sergeant Bob Thompson is going to climb under this van to attach the bird dog and I'm going to cover him as he is under the vehicle. The owner has a large dog so we bring some recently issued pepper spray that neither of us have used before. Bob successfully gets the bird on the van and we are walking east on 12th Avenue when Bob decides he wants to try this spray out and sprays it in the air. The wind is in our face causing the spray to come right back into Bob's eyes and he is blinded. I had to lead him back to his car by the hand. We had a good laugh but never tried it again. The pepper or OC spray is very effective on most but not all people but if you use it in an enclosed room there is a chance that everyone will be affected, not just the bad guy.

* * *

It's about 1 pm and I'm working with Brad Prentice when Sergeant Bob calls me on the radio and requests that I go to the office and prepare to do a cell mate. He tells me a guy around my age has just done a robbery on Victoria Drive where he shot and wounded a retired policeman. Brad and I return to the office and I start working on my cover story. We decide that I will be a bit of a rounder, not a big time crook but shady and I had just killed someone as a result of drunk driving. I go to the Empress Hotel beer parlor which is just across the lane from the police station and I down two glasses of beer and intentionally spill a little on my clothes. Then Brad wires me for sound with a body pack taped to my chest and back. Recently the courts had ruled this form of investigation would not be allowed unless it was used for safety reasons only and taping of the conversation was definitely out. This guy was supposed to be dangerous; he just shot someone, so we felt justified in wiring me for sound. When a cell mate operation is done the cell mate is given the minimum amount of information about the criminal cell mate while the handler or cover person is provided more details. He wants the cell mate to find out as much as he can without leading the bad guy into conversation.

Brad takes me up to the jail in handcuffs and when the elevator door opens I see this big guy in the holding cage near the booking desk. He is alone and I figure this is my guy. I look around and I don't recognize any of the jail guards except Sergeant Dan Dureau who is standing far away. The jail guard decides to book me in before the suspect so the guard comes around to my side of the counter and starts telling me what to do. The guard is a young redheaded police officer who may have been on the job for three years and he is now doing his mandatory year in the jail. He has never seen me before. All the time I am being booked into the jail the suspect in the holding cage is watching me. The young guard tells me to take off my boots, my mackinaw and then my sweatshirt. I am wearing a black T-shirt and I'm getting a little nervous with the excessive search as I thought these guys should know who I am and be aware of the operation and of my coming up to the jail. The guard then starts frisking me and feels the wire on my back that leads to the body pack taped to the small of my back. The guard said "What's this?" Dan Dureau steps in just in time and tells the young guard it's ok. I am allowed to put my clothes and boots back on. The guard leads me away to the end cell block that has about six large cells in it and he opens the big cell door and says I can be in which ever cell I want. There isn't a soul in the block. This guard now knows who I am and I tell him I will take the very first cell and to place the suspect in here with me. Unlike my first cell mate where there was one upper and lower bunk, this cell has both individual bunks on either side of the cell.

I am lying on my bunk having tested the body pack to see if it's working when the iron cell door to the cell block opens and the suspect is led into my cage. The guard closes the cell door and then walks through the iron door and locks it behind him. My cell mate is a big man about 48 years old and easy 250 pounds. He has a heavy accent but his English is fine. Naturally I am smoking as the smokes are my bait if I need them. It doesn't take long and the suspect asks me why I'm there. I tell him I'm in trouble because I was drinking and ran down someone and I think I may have killed them. I ask him why he is there and he tells me he robbed a bank. He says "I'm in big trouble". With that he wouldn't shut up. We were quite comfortable, each sitting on our own beds and he is telling me his life story. He escaped from a prison outside of

Edmonton 2 or 3 weeks ago with another guy and they worked their way out west. He tells me the two of them stole a car about a week ago from behind a church on Kingsway and Inman in Burnaby where it was left running by the lady who had gone inside the church. As they were driving away in the stolen car he said he looked around and there was a baby sitting in a car seat at the back of the vehicle. He and his partner didn't want to hurt the child and dropped the kid off on a door step on Boundary Road. I told my cellmate that I remember hearing about that on the news. The iron door opens and the guard comes for me. I leave the cell and report back to Brad. He says he is picking things up ok from my body pack and I have a fast sandwich that Brad brought for me. I am about to go back to my cell when Brad says go and put some of the finger print cleaner on your hands.

I walk back into the cell and the suspect asks where I have been and I say getting finger printed and he says he thought so, he could smell the soap. We start talking again and he tells me things didn't go well during the robbery today and some old guy got in the way and he shot him by accident and he was arrested near the bank. When the cell mate concluded I returned to the office to make my notes of the case and I used the tapes for the times when things were said while I was in the cell. The case went to trial some time later and Brad and I were not popular with the courts as they didn't think we should be using a wire at all. I know cell mates continued after that but I don't think any wire taping was allowed.

* * *

Its summer time and we are low on manpower because people are away on holidays so we have combined both Strike Force squads into one for a couple of weeks. We have been given a couple of commercial B&E guys to work on, Kerry Lamier and Garth Stein who live in North Vancouver. Detective Bill Parnell is the senior Detective so he is the road boss on this file as both Sergeants are away on holidays.

We set up on Lamier's apartment on West Keith Road. Lamier exits the apartment and gets into an old pick up truck and drives north on Delbrook to Stein's house. Stein leaves his house, gets into the old pick up truck and they both drive south on Delbrook and eventually across the Lions Gate Bridge and into Vancouver. It's around 8 pm and a beautiful summer evening and the two guys drive to Gastown; a trendy area that has small shops, bars and restaurants and they park their truck. They go night clubbing and move from one bar to another. About 1 am Lamier and Stein leave the bar and drive to a pizza restaurant on Robson Street where they meet a couple of girls. Most of us start suggesting to Bill Parnell, the Road Boss that these guys are chasing girls and not in a crime mode and we should call it a night. Bill will have nothing to do with our idea and we are staying with the file.

About 2:15 am Stein and Lamier exit the restaurant, say goodbye to the girls and get in their truck. Just when we think they may be going home they go to the Shell gas station at Burrard and Davie and gas up. Remember, this is a positive sign. After gassing up they start driving south across the Burrard Street Bridge and then turn right and park on the north side of 5th Avenue at Burrard Street. I am working with Brad Prentice and I'm driving a black Pontiac Trans Am. I drop Brad off near their location and I go and set up a block to the west at 5th and Cypress for takeaway. We have several feet out, a few cars set up for the take down and a couple of cars set for take away should they drive away from the area. One of the feet said the suspects are looking at a gun store on the west side of Burrard and then he advises they're now inside the shop.

Stein and Lamier come running out of the gun shop carrying what looks like five rifles with ammunition as well. They jump in their truck with Stein driving and Bill Parnell attempts to block the front of their truck while Brad Prentice is running to the passenger side of the truck. I can see what's happening from the corner of 5th and Cypress and it looks like all hell is breaking loose. The suspects speed away in their truck towards my location with their headlights out and take off the front of Bills car, my favorite grey Buick Regal. Bill had tried to box them in for a Tactical Vehicle Takedown. The two suspects then knocked Brad over with the side of their truck. I pull the Trans Am into the middle of the intersection of 5th and Cypress to block them and I can hear their truck speeding up and going through the changing of gears. I begin to think this isn't such a good idea and pull my car off the road. The suspects go by me west on 5th Avenue at about 90 km/h dragging the front end of Bill's grey Buick followed shortly by Bill driving what is left of his car. I start to parallel the chase from 4th Avenue as Bill is calling out his direction.

The other Strike Force cars are picking up our feet and are well behind us. Bill advises they are now westbound in a lane and the suspects are throwing things out the windows. I can see the dust from the dry gravel laneway forming in the air from 4th Avenue as the other two vehicles are going down the lane. I change channels to a Patrol radio and request some help advising that we are attempting to stop these guys and have no emergency equipment.

The radio operator advises me that she has help on the way but I have to keep her posted on our location. Bill is doing a great job but understandably he's getting pretty excited. I tell Bill that Patrol is trying to catch up and to try and stay with them. With my talking to both Patrol and Bill, I am constantly switching radio channels, still trying to drive fast at the same time and now I have lost sight of Bill. I know Bill took the Marine Drive cut off from 4th Avenue and then into an area called Jericho Circle. I just get to Marine and Discovery when both the suspects truck and Bill appear coming towards me from the opposite direction. They continue west on Marine Drive and I turn around to catch up. I have been advised by Radio that the University RCMP have been advised and they will assist and that a Vancouver Patrol car is not far behind us. The suspects continue driving west on North West Marine Drive into the University Endowment Lands and I can see a cloud of dust as the truck veers to the right towards the bushes. Bill advises they have dumped the truck and both suspects ran into the bushes towards Wreck Beach and the water of Burrard Inlet. Bill continues west past the abandoned pickup truck and sets up a perimeter to the west and I stop just before the truck and maintain a perimeter to the east.

The marked Patrol unit arrives within a minute followed by the rest of the Strike Force members. We have a dog man coming from Vancouver and another from the West Vancouver Police.

It is pitch black out with bush on either side of the road and we know they took guns from the gun store. While we saw them throw some away they may still have some left. We sit and wait. The dogs search for sometime and it's heavy going for them with pretty dense brush. After about an hour one of the dogs finds Stein hiding under a bunch of bushes. We could hear him screaming from the roadway when the dog caught him. The search continues for Lamier. It's getting light out and several hours have gone by since they dumped the truck and there is no sign of Lamier.

Things are starting to wrap up here as we request a tow truck for the suspect's pickup truck and a wagon for Stein. Brad and I decide to retrace the chase route to look for evidence. Since I was the closest to Bill in the chase I have a pretty good idea the route they took. As we are retracing the chase and driving east in the lane near Waterloo Street, we find two shot guns lying on the gravel laneway. We continue west for several blocks and find the front end of Bill's Buick. We move it over to the side and will have to get it later as it's too big to get into the hatchback of our Trans Am. It might be 5:30 am when Brad and I are nearing the scene of the crime driving north on Cypress Street around 7th Avenue. There is a tall good looking blonde guy walking south on Cypress from 6th Avenue and he has his sweater around his shoulders and light colored pants. You can almost hear the squishing sound from his wet shoes as he is walking. It's Kerry Lamier, we couldn't believe it. He had walked along the waters edge all the way from Wreck Beach to Kits Beach. We continue to drive by and not stare in his direction in order to not alert him. I drive around the block and then slowly approach from the north behind Lamier as he is walking south on Cypress. As I get closer Brad jumps out of the car followed by me right behind. Brad tackles Lamier and after a little rough stuff Lamier is hand cuffed and placed under arrest. A police wagon comes for him and Lamier tells us where the remainder of the stolen guns were thrown. Brad and I returned to the same lane where we found the first two guns and right at a curve in the lane, where they would have to have slowed down, are three more on top of the roof of a small shed. Everything was accounted for and no serious harm done to anyone except for the Buick. I think that was the end of that car.

* * *

I arrive at the Strike Force office one Friday afternoon to prepare for our afternoon shift and learn that the other Strike Force squad is still out on the road working on Ivan Stumpell, a 40 year old bank robber who is out on parole and living in a half way house in New Westminster. The other squad has a new Sergeant that doesn't really seem cut out for this type of work. They had been following Ivan and the new Sergeant had the eye when Ivan got through a light but the Sergeant stopped when the light turned red. The Sergeant would not run the red light when it was safe because that was illegal and Ivan was gone. Ivan ended up robbing a bank that afternoon at 70th and Granville but something went wrong and he only got $200. We are advised that the other squad has Ivan and some friends at a house on Alberta Road in Richmond, a community just south of Vancouver's city limits and policed by the RCMP. We are to get there and do a rollover and take over the file and continue the surveillance as we believe he will do another bank robbery.

To complete a rollover it takes a lot of time and it sometimes gets complicated. The other squad has all the Strike Force cars and heavy artillery such as shot guns or MP5's, which is an assault rifle. We drive to Richmond in regular unmarked police cars and find a house on #4 Road that has a large parking area and decide with the home owner's permission to use that as our base. The roll over is done one position at a time in case the suspect moves while we're in the process of changing personnel. We send a foot replacement and then their man returns. Then we send a car to replace theirs and they return to our position and so on. This process can sometimes take up to an hour to complete. We are half way through this process when Ivan and two other guys come out to an older van and drive away. We have the five Strike Force cars doing the surveillance and three unmarked police cars following well behind. There are probably 17 Strike Force members involved, twice the normal number because they moved during the rollover and both squads are mixed together. Ivan and his friends drive to Vancouver and down to West Broadway where they drive around a bit. They eventually go to the McDonald's Restaurant at Balaclava and Broadway where all three guys go inside to eat. We have a break to try and complete our rollover.

It's a Friday about 6pm and the banks have closed. We figure they are planning something for the next day and while the other squad is still here we are asking who might be available to work overtime on Saturday if the boss allows it. While we're in the discussion, Ivan and friends exit McDonald's and drive away in the van. They drive south on Balaclava and then east on 10th Avenue and then into a lane. We have an eye out and he says it looks like Ivan and another guy are changing into different clothes in the laneway. Once they have changed clothes they drive west in the lane, out to Broadway and then west as they slow down past a Credit Union in the 3300 block that appears to be still open for business. The Credit Union is located immediately to the west of the McDonald's Restaurant they were just at. The van pulls into the lane and parks in an open area behind the Credit Union. Jim Mackin has got an eye on the Credit Union from across the street and Vicki Matheson has worked her way up to the top of a fire escape behind the Credit Union and over looking the parked van.

Sergeant Bob Thompson has taken over command from the previous Sergeant and we have all the cars set up for a possible take down. Ivan and another male exit the van and start walking towards Broadway leaving the getaway driver in the parked van at the rear of the credit union. When they get to Broadway they look inside the Credit Union but walk west on Broadway away from the Credit Union. Ivan is looking very sporty wearing a ball cap and a grey team style jacket with leather sleeves. Jim Mackin says they have turned around and are heading back. Sergeant Bob says if they do the robbery we will move in as soon as they get back to the van which is facing east in the lane. I think this is the first time that Sergeant Bob has made a quick decision. Jim says they have entered the bank and Jim's voice gets excited when he says they have the customers on the floor and they have jumped the counter. Jim calls them out of the bank and running towards the lane. Vickie advises they are almost at the van and we start to move in. I am driving the Pontiac Trans Am and I am to come in from the east end of the lane and head-on to stop the van from exiting the lane. I drive slowly into the lane so as to not show our hand as other cars are coming in from the west end of the lane to be behind the van. The van is blocked and we now have a Mexican standoff. I jump out of my car and forget to put it into park as it continues to roll forward towards the van. I am able to get back inside and stop it. There is a bunch of screaming going on. The van is surrounded on all sides by police with all kinds of weaponry all pointed at Ivan but at each other as well. Ivan is waving this gun around with the side sliding door of the van open but he eventually drops the gun and he and the other two suspects exit the van and lie down on the ground as instructed. I hand cuff Ivan and I have never seen a scarier looking guy. His eyes were steel grey and I could see that he would like to kill me if he could.

We were very lucky things went as they did. The cross fire threat was unbelievable and had Ivan started shooting it could have been ugly for a lot of us. Jim and Vicki did a great job, in particular Vicki who was in a very vulnerable position at the top of the fire escape and I thought she showed great courage through this ordeal. I think that file finished her though because I don't think she was ever gung ho again.

I went to the Remand Court a couple of days later to see what was going to happen to Ivan. The Sheriffs cleared the court and Ivan was brought out in hand cuffs and leg irons. Since Ivan was already on day parole for robbery the Judge gave him another 18 years to be added on to his current sentence. Ivan broke down and told the Judge he will be an old man by the time he gets out. This was a pretty stiff penalty compared to most sentences.

* * *

Because of the nature of the work and the evidence that is required to convict someone of a crime, the Strike Force will usually let the crime happen and then arrest the person immediately afterword. Until the bank robber has actually handed the robbery note to the teller there is no crime and it's pretty difficult to prove his intent as he may change his mind at the last minute. There are some situations however that may be so dangerous we could not let the offence take place.

We are working on a bank robber living around 22nd and Rupert and he has shot someone in the past at a drug store robbery. We have reliable information that he most likely has a gun and is planning a bank robbery. It's the winter time and there is a small amount of snow on the ground. Our bank robber teams up with a little Hispanic guy who owns a small white Toyota. After driving around the better part of the day the two suspects arrive at the Bank of Montreal at Rupert and Grandview Highway. The main suspect gets out and the driver goes and parks at the rear of the bank. It is quickly decided that if the main guy walks to the front door of the bank he will be taken down hard and the same for the Hispanic in the car. Sure enough the guy goes to the front door and two of our guys take him down hard. In the meantime Jim Mackin and Scott Hume have moved in to take down the getaway driver in the lane. I pull into the lane and here are Jim and Scott struggling with the little Hispanic trying to get him out of the car. I get out of my car to help because I can't understand why they are having so much trouble with this little guy. The problem turned out to be that the guy still has his seat belt on. The hard take down was a little delayed on him. We didn't like arresting our bank robber this way but we didn't think we could take any chances because of his violent past, even though we knew there was a good chance the case would be thrown out. The guy had the note and the gun and considering his record the Crown accepted the charges.

I have decided to enter the Sergeants promotional competition and start studying for the exam. With the experience I have learned while in the Strike Force I have decided I would make a good

Sergeant and had the support of my Inspector, Staff Sergeant and new Sergeant, Wayne Meyers.

* * *

It's a few days before Christmas 1990 and the entire Vice Section, Strike Force, Drug Squad and Vice Intelligence is having a Christmas party. We pay for the party ourselves, about $50 per couple and we have rented a nice hall at Main and 15th Avenue. Around 5 pm I have just got my newly purchased suit on, I'm having a drink and my wife has gone to get the babysitter. The telephone rings and it's my boss Wayne Meyers saying we have been called into work and the Christmas party is cancelled for our squad. Wayne tells me a well known successful Vancouver businessman's daughter has been kidnapped and we are required at the office right away. No sooner do I hang up the phone and my wife walks in with the babysitter. I tell her what has happened and to take the sitter home while I get changed out of my suit and into some work clothes. I am on my way to the office within 10 minutes.

When I arrive at the office the husband of the victim is sitting there with one of the Major Crime Detectives and I unlock all the equipment as our squad members start to arrive. The Sergeant, Wayne Meyers and I go down to the Major Crime office where a briefing is taking place. The victim's husband has received a ransom note demanding a huge some of money, around $200,000 - $300,000. The note also states that the victim is buried somewhere and they have supplied a straw which allows her to breathe. The suspects say there will be further contact with the victim's husband.

Sometime later the husband is contacted by the kidnappers and told to be at the Hudson's Bay Store at Georgia and Granville where a table is set up near the lower level. The husband is to place the money in a brief case under the table. The kidnapper also says there will be people watching the victim if something should go wrong. The main objective is to get the victim back alive but we have to follow the suspect hoping he will lead us to her. We have feet out in and around the store but we have to be careful as we have no idea who we are looking for or how many. I have grabbed a parking spot on Seymour Street facing north right in front of the Bay Department Store in case I'm needed. My foot is Brad Prentice and he is in the store some place. When the feet get into the store and start to go to the basement level the cars have difficulty picking up their radio transmissions.

The store is very close to closing for the night and I hear that the victim's husband has arrived and placed the brief case with the money under the specified table and then left the area. Now we wait. A couple of minutes go by and then I hear Bruce Waters yelling the suspect has got the brief case and he has gone down towards the lower mall which can lead to Howe or Granville Streets. Bruce has lost him for a few minutes and then I hear him transmit that the guy is carrying a back pack and is headed north in the lower mall. Downtown Vancouver has a lot of one way streets so I head over to Howe Street, a one way for southbound traffic, and a possible exit for the kidnapper. As I am just turning onto Howe Street from Dunsmuir I hear someone transmit that the suspect has just exited the mall onto Howe Street. As I am driving south on Howe Street the suspect is running north on the east sidewalk against vehicular traffic. I broadcast his location and I move over to Hornby Street, a one way street north bound and now I see the suspect running south on the west sidewalk against traffic.

Brad Prentice has the suspect in the breezeway of the Vancouver Hotel and getting into a Yellow Taxi cab. The taxi drives away, Brad gets back into my car and we follow the vehicle with the suspect sitting in the back seat and who appears to be changing his clothes. The taxi drives west on Georgia from Burrard and then south on Bute, he turns right to go west on Alberni Street and then south on Jervis Street where the suspect gets out and enters the Palisades Hotel, 1200 block Robson Street. We have all our feet out and someone says they think they saw him in the hotel lobby and maybe take the elevator up. We never see the suspect again. We sit on the hotel and go through what everyone saw and try and determine where he went. We have every room in the hotel checked starting at the top and working down. We are instructed if

we do see the suspect to take him down and not follow him
anymore. In fact a plan was in the making from the high command
of taking the suspect to Stanley Park for interrogation if necessary.
We knew at the outset this wasn't going to be easy but we felt
terrible. We had lots of opportunity to take the kidnapper down
but that wasn't the plan and now our pride is shot because we
didn't do the job expected of us. We are still sitting around the
hotel around 5 or 6 am when we are contacted on the police radio
that the victim has been released unharmed. We are grateful for
that and return to the office still wishing to have had a piece of the
kidnapper.

I am now home relaxing after a short sleep and watching the news
on the television and see that our brilliant kidnappers got arrested
in West Vancouver at the Park Royal Mall. They had been
throwing money around and had rented a limousine for shopping.
The Limo driver thought something was wrong and called the
West Vancouver Police who arrested them. We lost our Christmas
party but made some overtime and the victim was returned
unharmed so not all was lost.

* * *

As you can see, things don't always go as planned and sometimes
we are riding blind. We are given a file where a robbery is
suspected to take place at the home of a wealthy business owner
who lives in the exclusive Shaughnessy district. The suspect has
been identified and is living out in Surrey. The information we
received from the informant is the potential victim, Mr. Wang,
keeps all the proceeds from the business at his home and the
suspect or an associate of the suspect saw Mr. Wang counting the
money in his home office and they plan on robbing him at the
house. Sergeant Wayne Meyers and I drive to the victim's house
while the rest of the squad go to Surrey and set up on the suspect's
residence. The victim's house is a large estate with a swimming
pool in the back and a brick wall around the entire property.
Wayne and I want to talk with the victim and warn him of the
potential danger ahead but there is no answer at the door. We walk

around the back and check all the doors and everything appears secure. We have called the business but neither Mr.Wang nor his eldest son is there.

Wayne and I decide to go to the neighbor and enquire if they know where Mr. Wang or his family might be. The neighbor tells us they don't really know the Wang family but they share the same gardener, Guido, and he may know where they are. The neighbor gives me Guido's phone number. I advise the squad in Surrey we cannot locate Mr. Wang but I'm about to call Guido the gardener and I'll get back to them. I phone Guido and tell him my name and that I'm a Detective from the Vancouver Police, I don't say the Strike Force, and that we are trying to located either Mr. Wang or his son about an important family matter and does he know how we can contact them? Guido says he has no idea where they may be and asks if everything is all right and I tell him it is and we hang up.

Within two minutes we can hear our members in Surrey are mobile with the suspect. They are driving south on the King George Highway and the suspect is doing unbelievable heat checks and he eventually just pulls over and lets our cars drive by. It turns out Guido the gardener was the associate who was setting the robbery up and had been the one to see the victim counting the money in the victim's home office. After my phone call to him he called the suspect who was going to do the actual robbery to warn him. Naturally the robbery never took place as they knew we were on to them and I got quite a ribbing from the squad for calling Guido on the phone. We had a laugh over it. It just went to show, you have to be careful who you talk to even though they seem to be OK they just might hinder your investigation.

We had a similar situation a few months earlier in the Strike Force when we were working on an arsonist on the east side of Vancouver. The suspect was a young kid about 19 years old and we had his name and address written on the blackboard with all our plans on working on him. Things never happened and it turned out that the cleaning lady who cleaned our office was the mother of a girl who was dating the suspect. The cleaning lady passed along our information to her daughter and the file was over. The cleaning lady was a very nice person who almost got fired over the incident; instead she was no longer allowed to work in any sensitive areas. It's a tough call because most parents would have said something to their daughter if only to tell her to stay away from this idiot.

* * *

In the Strike Force there were a lot of hockey fans in particular Vancouver Canuck fans. I enjoyed hockey but I never played the game and I could barely skate. One of the guys arranges a game with the Police Hockey Team. Brian Burke, the hockey guru and Assistant GM for Vancouver at the time was a member of that team. We show up at the rink in east Vancouver and everyone on both teams seemed to have their own hockey equipment. I was given a helmet, shin pads and a hockey stick. Over this expensive equipment I was wearing was a red and black mackinaw shirt and grey sweatpants. The rules of the game were no slap shots. I was floundering around on the ice trying to stand up let alone try and contribute to the team. I remember being near the goalie where I probably shouldn't have been and Burke let go with a blistering wrist shot that just missed my head. I thought this game could be fun if you knew how to skate but I was out of my league. At least I was prepared to give it a try but I wished they played Rugby.

* * *

After a Vancouver Canucks Hockey game, two guys, one of them in a wheel chair, went to the bar at Broadway and Hemlock for a drink. There was some kind of altercation inside the club over a female between the able bodied friend and a Pilipino male. The staff kicked the Pilipino guy out of the bar for the night. When the other guy and his wheel chair bound friend left the bar, the man who was thrown out earlier was waiting outside for them. He shot and killed the man while he was wheeling out his companion in the wheel chair to their vehicle in the parking lot.

Perhaps a week later the Major Crime Section had a suspect in mind and gave us a possible address and to see if we could follow him. We followed the suspect who was with a Pilipino female. We believed the two lived together in the basement suite and the subject was driving the female to work. We followed them for some time which eventually led us to the area of Grandville Island. The subject began making moves that made us think we may have been burnt.

The Major Crime Detective in charge of the case said to arrest him and bring him in. As the suspect stopped at a stop sign on Lamey's Mill Road we did a tactical vehicle takedown where you block the subjects vehicle from the front and the back so he can't move. He was believed to be armed and dangerous so we weren't taking any chances. The subject didn't respond to the commands of our first guy at his door so we used a baseball bat to take out the driver's side car window. We hadn't used this before and it proved to be very effective and it did get everyone's attention. The female passenger was screaming of course, the suspect looked shit scared and they were both covered in broken glass. Unfortunately this was about 10:30 am and there was a bus slowly driving by with a load of shocked passengers looking out the window at what they would have thought to be a bunch of bearded, long haired thugs beating the shit out of this car with a nice couple inside it. After the male and female were taken away we executed a search warrant at the suspect's basement suite and found the gun used in the homicide under a cushion in an over stuffed arm chair. The next morning we learned that the suspect had hanged himself in the jail before he could first appear in the Remand Court.

I write my Sergeants exam and receive good and bad news. I passed the exam but my two years in the Strike Force is up and I'm being transferred to the jail as a Corporal. The time in the Strike Force was exciting but I was feeling burnt out and knew it was time for a rest. I will do my jail time and continue with the promotion process which includes an interview and maybe I will be promoted before my jail time is up.

The Let Down

Everyone is required to do their inside time and they will get you sooner or later. Normally you will do some inside time shortly after you first become a policeman and then again soon after you get promoted. I never did my jail time but I volunteered to work the Fraser Street Police Office and I was told that would count in place of working in the jail. I guess it didn't count because here I am in the jail. Some members would have done their jail time as a constable and then if they got promoted maybe go to Communications. I was probably lucky. The jail has some permanent Custodial Guards, an on duty nurse, a cook and about five police officers per shift.

The walls of the jail are painted a mellow green colour and there are three floors, the 4th, 5th and 6th floor. The 4th floor is for the women prisoners and the jail nurse, the 5th floor for the men and the 6th floor for immigration prisoners and the kitchen. Members assigned to the jail do not carry any weapons and in fact, as soon as a police officer brings in a prisoner he is to put his weapon into a locked locker before doing anything further. The last thing you want is to have a weapon taken from you in these tight quarters. The elevator is now automatic and operated by a member behind a desk, no more Frank hiding behind his book pretending he didn't hear or see anything and the brass railing inside the elevator has been removed. There are video cameras all over the jail and you need a jail key to go anywhere. The jail is self contained so when you are working in the jail you don't leave until your shift is over unless it's for something special, and that applies to everyone, Constable or NCO.

The Vancouver jail only holds the prisoners until they can appear in court the next day or they are released by the Justice of the Peace on a weekend if the offence is minor and the prisoner meets all the criteria for release. Immigration prisoners may be required to stay several days for a deportation hearing and they are lodged on a different floor than the regular prisoners.

The jail runs pretty smoothly but it's a depressing place to work. The evening and night shifts can be pretty wild, particularly Friday and Saturday nights with the intoxicated males and females that are brought in. The jail has had a lot of history and as a result of several enquiries and court cases, there are cameras positioned throughout the jail in the event of any future complaints.

As an NCO I have an office in the jail. The office has a window looking outside and several windows looking inside the jail and towards the booking desk. Besides being in charge of the jail I am also responsible for proof reading all the reports on the arrested prisoners to ensure all the essential elements for the arrest are in the report. I am also responsible for changing the video tapes for the 5 or 6 cameras installed in the jail to record any disturbances or acts of abuse, real or conjured up.

This is one place in my career I hated working. You could leave home having had a nice dinner, change into your uniform in the main building, walk over to the jail and ride up the elevator in a good mood. Just before you get to the 5th floor you start hearing the fighting and yelling and then the elevator door opens and this is home for the next eight hours.

I have my interview for the Sergeant's competition with a Superintendant and two Inspectors. It's all very formal as you salute the Superintendant when you enter the room and you are dressed in your best uniform. Each of the three member panel will ask you questions or give you a scenario that you are to solve or comment on. It can be quite challenging but I think I did pretty well.

* * *

One day in the Jail one of the Inspectors from my Sergeant's interview has an occasion to be near the booking desk and he tells me the Department is going to make five Sergeants this year and he congratulates me because I am number five on the list. That news uplifted my spirits and I figure I'll get through this jail time.

A few days later the promotional list comes out and my name is not on it. One of the contestants went to the Promotional Board after the competition was over and received another point for taking a History course and that left me ½ point behind and out of the competition.

I didn't handle it well! I don't like losing and I don't like rejection. I figure I had been jobbed out of this promotion and at the very least they should make six Sergeants. I was told by the Staff Sergeant in charge of Staff Development that if I make too much of a fuss it could hurt me and they may not add on to the list this year, which they often did. But no, I couldn't let it go. I couldn't keep my big mouth shut. I went to the Union and filed a grievance that the process had been flawed, which it had, but I was only digging a bigger hole for myself. I think one of my biggest concerns was I studied so hard for the exam and we all know studying isn't my strong suit. I was so close and now I have to write the exam again next year. This process was changed a couple of years later so that your exam mark will be good for three years but that was too late for me.

The timing for this rejection wasn't good. Had I still been in the Strike Force or a Detective out on the road I may have handled it better but I hated where I was working and I was trapped inside these green walls fuming and bitter and no way to vent my frustrations.

* * *

While working in the jail I got my first glimpse of the new breed of officers coming on the job. I thought they had been watching too many American 'cop' movies and were a little too cocky for their tenure. Two young male constables were showing me this police magazine where it displayed this huge emergency light bar for the top of the patrol car and some police uniforms and weighted gloves. I told them I thought there were more important things to worry about than lighting up the sky with this light bar but they knew best. I saw them a couple of years later walking the beat on Robson Street in the summertime wearing their short sleeve uniform shirts and black gloves. I thought they looked goofy and were trying to look tough.

* * *

I never knew who I might see from my office when the Jail elevator door opened. One day a guy I played Junior Big Four football with and who eventually played professionally for the BC Lions, was brought in for money laundering. I don't think he recognized or remembered me. Another time they brought in a well known female who had been a secretary at one time for the Police Department. She was pretty drunk and had been involved in a minor accident and the officers had no choice but to arrest her. The worst was one afternoon the door opened and there was my old partner John Hossack from Team 6. John had quit the job several years earlier, got divorced and he was here over some problem with his girl friend. I guess some things never change. I went and got him a coffee and I sat in the cell with him for awhile and talked.

* * *

I had one new officer work for me in the jail that just drove me nuts. I think I would like to have taken him out to the back alley myself. This guy was hired when he was 40 years old and had been on the job about 3 years before coming to the jail. This guy worked with Larry Holbrook from the Motorcycle Drill Team after

Larry got transferred to District 4. Larry himself was pretty laid back but this guy was way too laid back.

When I arrived at work one night the Corporal from the previous shift tells me they have Steven Crawly, a well know thug from the skids, hog tied in one of the quiet rooms. I have dealt with Steven when I was on the Strike Force and know what a fighter he is. Now these quiet rooms are very small and claustrophobic with no windows or bars but a solid metal door. To be hog tied, hands and feet tied behind your back together, is not very comfortable. I can hear Steven screaming from my office but I tune him out because he obviously hasn't slowed down. My problem Constable Kyle wants to let Steven out of the quiet room. I would say "no, not yet", but Kyle would persist. Finally I said, "OK Kyle but if he rips your face off don't look at me for help". Kyle let him out, partially untied Steven and moved him to a different cell without incident. I told Kyle after that he should be transferred to the Skids in District 2 where he can learn something about policing instead of being in Sleepy Hollow in District 4. He was probably transferred back to District 4 and continued to be useless.

I get a phone call one day from Staff Development. I have another 2 ½ months of jail time to go but it can always go longer. Staff Development wants to talk to me about my union grievance and I tell them I will drop it if they transfer me out of the jail. I know some people have won their grievances in the past and I had a good chance of winning mine. I thought if they don't want to promote me especially after all my fuss, my career could be hell anyway. Its one thing to be a Constable and be tarnished but you don't want to be an NCO with that reputation. We agree I will be transferred to the Coordinated Law Enforcement Unit (C.L.E.U.) and I will drop my grievance.

Much Ado, About Nothing

In February 1992 I am transferred to CLEU and specifically the Asian Crime Section. There were two other units in CLEU, Unit C, a Fraud Section and Unit B, a general surveillance section but the Asian Crime Unit was the largest section with two teams and an Intelligence section specifically for Asian criminals. Part of the reason that I was transferred here, besides appeasing my grievance, was my developed expertise in surveillance I learned from the Strike Force. In the area of surveillance I was very good at my job.

CLEU was first formed in 1974 by the Provincial Government to attack numerous cross boundary major crimes in the Lower Mainland. Until then Vancouver Police may not be aware of crimes in West Vancouver or Richmond communities and vice-versa. By coordinating all the police forces with their members working together, information was expected to be shared more readily. It may have worked when CLEU was first implemented but it didn't seem to be working now.

The largest amount of man power comes from the biggest police forces so Vancouver Police and the RCMP had the majority of members in CLEU. Then there were a few members from Delta Police, New Westminster Police and West Vancouver Police. There was a similar operation on Vancouver Island called the Joint

Forces Operation that used the RCMP and the various Island Police Departments.

In my view the problem was protectionism. It was hard to figure out who was the boss. Every unit had a Vancouver Staff Sergeant and an RCMP Staff Sergeant and they would share an office. If you had an RCMP Sergeant you had to have at least two Vancouver Detectives in the squad. Reports were filled out by the Mounties one way and the Municipal members another. RCMP members could take holidays a day at a time where Vancouver had to take it at a minimum of a week at a time. You could never keep track of anybody and I don't think anyone cared. It seemed to me they were trying to fit a bunch of square pegs into round holes; people doing jobs that they were not really suited or qualified for.

* * *

I start off in Asian Crime and I work with Ian Hart who is a member of the Vancouver Police. Ian is a good guy, an excellent policeman with a great sense of humor who has a million jokes. Ian loves what he is doing here at CLEU and he is trying to teach me their routine. I can tell Ian hasn't done a lot of REAL surveillance but he knows his Asian crooks.

Ian didn't like to admit it but he was as blind as a bat and wouldn't wear glasses. I'm the new guy so Ian is driving the unmarked car and he takes me to a house that we are to be watching. Unlike the Strike Force, we are working on our own without any backup. Ian parallel parks the car one house away from the suspect's house and on the same side of the street. This is not the thing to do. Then Ian reaches into the back seat and pulls out some binoculars and starts watching the house that is forty yards away. No sooner have I voiced my concern to Ian about his eye sight and how it might not be wise to be this close than the suspect from the house comes out, walks to my side of the car and asks what we are doing. Ian made up some story and we got the hell out of there.

When you are doing surveillance you don't want anyone to know why you're there, especially the bad guy. Ian and I are following a suspect along Oak Street and we are both in separate cars. I can see some people staring at Ian as they are passing him in the fast lane. I notice that Ian is holding the microphone for the radio up to his mouth when he's talking. If you're in uniform and in a marked police car this is the proper way of using the radio but not doing surveillance. I suggest it might be better to hold the microphone in his lap so no one can see it, but Ian got mad and said he's done lots of surveillance and he doesn't need any help from me. There went the idea of sharing my surveillance expertise. It was a real mish mash there.

The Sergeant for our unit was a little guy who had been with the Mounties for about 30 years and they just brought him back from Hong Kong where he had been a Liaison Officer for some time. I don't think he had any idea of what was going on. We had been working on a restaurant that we believed was selling illegal cigarettes and one night Jack, the Sergeant advises he has found the evidence. We asked what he found and he said he found some empty large cigarette boxes in the dumpster at the rear of the restaurant. We had to tell the Sergeant that anyone could have put it there not to mention people use these boxes for all kinds of uses and the boxes he found were for domestic cigarettes and not imports that we were looking for. It was embarrassing.

Our particular squad had maybe eight people and I can't recall ever having us all work at the same time. Somebody was either off meeting some supposed informant or they were off to pipe band practice. We had one guy from Delta Police who was completely lost in what to do and I don't think anyone really tried to help him much. We would be watching a suspect's house for a few hours and when this member drove away there would be a pile two inches deep of sun flower seed shells on the road where he had been parked. Not something done doing surveillance.

* * *

One afternoon shift in the summer I show up for work and there is no one there. I mean no one. I make some phone calls and a couple of the guys have gone to Seattle to have a tour of a United

States aircraft carrier, some have taken a day's vacation and the rest have the usual excuses. I can't do anything on my own and call the Staff Sergeant at home to tell him how pissed off I am that no one bothered telling me they wouldn't be at work. I don't think he could have cared less.

* * *

A couple of slugs get transferred back to their own Department and Alex MacDonald from Vancouver and Dean Mitchell from the RCMP are transferred in. Based on some information we received, the three of us do surveillance on some Vietnamese guys. Alex and I are in one car and Dean is in another car by himself. Well our suspect picks up some buddies and they start driving around the west side of Vancouver obviously casing out some houses to break into. I phone the office and try and muster up some help as these guys are getting close to doing something and I think we might be getting a little warm with our two car surveillance. No one at the office could help. One guy was doing a performance appraisal on somebody and someone else was completing a police report. I thought because we worked Asian crime and these guys were Asian and about to do a break and enter someone might be interested. I was wrong. When I got back to the office I phoned the Vancouver Strike Force and I told them what I had seen and they got the guys breaking into a house the next day.

* * *

One night when there were actually about six of us together and we decide to check out this new Asian night club near Hornby and Pender Streets. We go inside and there are a lot of individual glass rooms and this place is all geared up as a Karaoke Bar. We sit down and order a drink and when the drinks come we are told they were bought by one of the crooks that owns the place. I didn't like this at all, particularly when I was told we had to buy them one back or else it would be considered an insult to Chinese customs. What a crock of shit I thought. As if that wasn't enough, Ian Hart asks me what I'm going to sing as he is looking through this Karaoke song book. I said "I'm not singing anything!" in an angry tone. "Oh." Ian says, "You have to sing something". He tells me he is going to sing A White Sports Coat, a Marty Robbins hit from the past. Ian gets up and sings and he is pretty good. I decide to go to the washroom and when I'm in there I can hear Glen Robinson bellowing out some off key song. I started to laugh. When it came to singing Glen was no Marty Robbins or even an Ian Hart. I couldn't handle it any more and left the club on my own and returned to the office.

The next day I received information from someone that the club that we had been in the night before was dealing in Marlborough Cigarettes which were not available for sale in Canada but an Asian favorite. I passed this on to one of the members that dragged us to the club in the first place and he said" I guess I should speak to them". I said I guess so or maybe even charge them.

* * *

I had begun to realize that where I am is a dumping ground with the very odd exception. It was my opinion that CLEU had gone from a unit that was respected to a place where the police departments could send the people they wanted to get rid of. I was obviously bitter and vocal over what happened over the Sergeant's competition and as CLEU was located at a separate location what better way to get rid of me, particularly when I said I would like to go there.

I have had enough of this and I go to see my old Inspector Al Grandia who is now in Staff Development and good guy. I tell Al that I want out of CLEU and we discuss the problems in getting a replacement. He tells me I should be going into the Sergeant's competition again for another try. I tell him there is no way I am going through the hours of studying for the exam again and retell my story of woe about getting cheated out of the promotion. My bitterness is rearing its ugly head again. Al Says" Doug, no one cares if you get promoted or not, they need a warm body for Sergeant and they will put someone else there if it's not you." I told Al I know that and that's why the Department has some screwed up supervisors because they are just filling the space with yes men and not qualified people. It was unfair of me to unleash on Al because it wasn't his fault I didn't get promoted or that I can be a hot head at times, but he was the figurehead sitting behind the Staff Development desk.

I don't get transferred out of CLEU but I am replaced by Bill Lu a Vancouver Detective who takes my spot in Asian Crime and I go to the Fraud Unit or from the frying pan into the fire.

* * *

In January 1993 I start in the CLEU Fraud Unit and the very first day we execute a search warrant on an apartment suite and the basement suite of a house. The unit has been working on this file for sometime before I got there so I have little knowledge of what is going on. We are to seize all the property out of both units because they are expected to have been purchased with stolen or forged credit cards. I am assigned to help Gary Rushton as Co-Exhibit men because there is so much property. The seized property included some very expensive watches and cameras worth thousands of dollars but the locked room we are keeping the property in is accessible by anyone who has a key and that included a lot of people. Gary and I spent months in this room with no windows or ventilation, tagging the property and eventually sending it downtown to the Vancouver Police Property Office. One day the suspects in this case who are now out of jail awaiting their court appearance, arrive at our office and are wishing to have some of their personal items taken during the seizure returned to them. Without Gary's or my knowledge one of the bosses goes down to our locked room and returns some property without our consent. Gary and I both raised our concerns to our Vancouver and RCMP Staff Sergeants about the lack of continuity with the seized evidence because non authorized people were being allowed into the room without our knowledge. The bosses both thought everything was fine. Sometime later after I had been transferred Gary told me a watch went missing from the room and the bosses made him the suspect. It was typical. The rules of evidence were pretty basic but we had some bosses who were academics and had no real police experience. They were round pegs in square holes.

I was a round peg in a square hole myself. I didn't belong there. I had no interest in fraud and half the time I didn't know what they were talking about. I told the boss that if I wanted to do Fraud cases I could have joined the Vancouver Police Fraud Squad but it's not for me. It didn't seem long ago that I had been living on the edge of excitement, getting dirty and arresting some big time crooks and here I am sitting behind a desk in the Fraud section at CLEU without any idea of what I'm doing.

* * *

That year there was a Summit meeting between President Clinton, Boris Yeltsin of Russia and the Canadian Prime Minister Brian Mulroney. It was all hands on deck, everyone was required to do something in regards to policing this event. Traffic members did their motorcycle escorts, ERT were designated snipers, there was the Crowd Control Unit on stand by and members doing overall security around the Pan Pacific Hotel and the Hyatt Hotel. What job did I get? I am assigned to directing traffic outside the Pan Pacific Hotel. I had to dust off my uniform that I hadn't worn in some time and hope that it would still fit. It was tight but I got into it. Here I am in uniform with my Corporal stripes directing traffic not far from the hotels door man. We're both in uniform but the door man is getting tips.

We are all putting in long 12 to 14 hour shifts for this Summit and the Vancouver members have to drive home to get some sleep and then return the next day for another tour of duty. The RCMP members have been brought in from around the country, but even those that live in the Lower Mainland get their own individual hotel room at some of the finest hotels all paid by the tax payer.

* * *

I can't help it but I'm not making a lot of friends at CLEU. Around September I get transferred to the surveillance unit, Unit B and while it still has its round pegs, its a little closer to what I know and understand.

This Unit had the potential of working on some good cases and we were often requested to assist other Departments in surveillance because they probably thought we knew what we were doing. Boy, were they wrong.

The team break down was similar to the other teams with the two Staff Sergeants, a Sergeant, Detectives and a smattering of Constables. Well, when it came to surveillance the Staff Sergeants didn't come along and that was probably a good thing because they would have been of little help. We had an RCMP and Vancouver Sergeant that occasionally did something with us but not much. We had one Constable that owned his own airplane that we used for surveillance and another that was the spotter in the plane. That didn't leave too many left on the ground. We had one Vancouver Detective that couldn't stay awake and always fell asleep reading the newspaper as he was holding the eye. The suspect would leave his house without the rest of us knowing only to have the suspect drive by us and we find out our guy in the eye is asleep or reading the newspaper.

I team up with Bob Delf, another Detective, and who is the son of my old Traffic Corporal Bob Delf Senior. We seemed to work pretty well together but I was definitely the bad guy in the good guy, bad guy partnership. I was the A personality while Bob was pretty laid back. While I seemed to always be the driver in the Strike Force, Bob liked to drive, so I didn't mind relaxing and being his foot when we needed it. Our man in the airplane really controlled the surveillance because without him we weren't very good. When he was around it worked beautifully. We could be blocks away from the suspect and he would never know he was being followed. But if it got cloudy or the plane needed refueling we were in trouble. At least I felt we were trying to accomplish something which seemed more than the other units.

* * *

One day Bob and I see a theft of tools from a parked car take place with a carload of young guys. We tried to enlist some other squad members for help but they were too busy. Bob is driving the blue Chevy Blazer that he always liked to drive. We follow the guys east on 33rd which is a two lane street. We are stuck in traffic at 33rd and Granville about two cars back of the suspects. My A personality takes over and I tell Bob to drive up on the wrong side of the road and pull up beside the stopped suspect's car and I will get out and pull the driver out of the car. Bob is reluctant but I yell at him to do it. Bob pulls up beside the suspect's driver's door and I can't open my door because we are too close to the car. The driver of the suspect's car looks at me and I look at him and he sees me trying to open my door and he's figured out who we are. The suspect driver turns his car to the right and drives off, over the curb, down the sidewalk and south on Granville. The car chase is on. We go down some lanes with speed bumps and Bob doesn't want to go too fast as the Blazer is top heavy. The Emergency beep tone is on the police radio as we broadcast our direction. We are only doing about 65km/h down the lane but a patrol supervisor tells us to call off the chase. We lost the guys anyway so now we have to go to the Oakridge Police Station to start filling out reports for calling "Code 4" on the radio and getting into a car chase. I don't think Bob was impressed but at least there had been a glimpse of excitement.

Not unlike the other units at CLEU there never seemed to be a full compliment of people around. Someone was always off doing something and we had a lot of senior people that had 6 and 7 weeks of holidays.

* * *

The Victoria Joint Forces Operation (JFO) has been working on a file on the Island involving drugs and the suspect has led them to Vancouver. Bob Delf and I are requested to assist in the surveillance of a male who has come to Vancouver to make a purchase of a kilo of Cocaine. The subject appeared to have made a large buy in the area of Seymour and Drake. As the day progresses their Road Boss asks Bob and I if the subject goes to

the Tsawwassen Ferry Terminal would we arrest him so they will
not blow their cover. We didn't want to get that involved but said
ok. Sure enough the subject goes to the Tsawwassen Ferry and
pays for the ferry to Vancouver Island. Bob and I flash our badges
to get past the ticket booth and get in the lineup and park several
cars behind the suspect in the same lane. The JFO guys are well
behind. As we are formulating our plan to make the arrest the
subject exits his Ford Mustang and begins to walk towards the
Terminal building. It is a cool afternoon and the wind is howling
at about 40 km/h. The subject is a white male in his 40's and
wears a metal leg brace and walks with a limp. Even with my
limp, I feel confident I can keep up with him. We approach the
subject and I identify ourselves as Vancouver Police and that he is
under arrest for Trafficking in a Narcotic. I gave the official
warning by memory and advised that he was not obliged to say
anything but anything he did say could be used in evidence, etc. I
hand cuff the subject and start walking him back towards his car. I
ask the subject to open his car and he naturally is reluctant. I must
have had a moment of Dirty Harry or something because I lost my
head and said "Give me your fucking keys" and grabbed the car
keys from his pocket. I looked inside the car and I could see a
brief case which we believed contained the drugs, sitting on the
rear floor behind the passenger seat. I entered the car and sure
enough there was the kilo of Cocaine inside the brief case.

The subject said he needed to go to the bathroom badly and would
we allow that. I said ok and after locking up his car with the
cocaine still inside we walked him over to the building that
contained the washrooms. My sensitive side came out and I
removed the handcuff from his right wrist and left his left hand
handcuffed to his belt. I made the subject keep the stall door open
while he was doing his business. At this point I thought I should
make sure I had the Official Warning correct and I decided to warn
the subject again. This time I read off the Department supplied
printed card and he was forced to listen while in the washroom
stall. I don't think Bob was impressed even though he was
laughing. The subject was taken to the Delta Police Station jail
and we did our reports with the Victoria guys who seemed
satisfied. It was at least two years before we went to court in

Victoria on this case. The Courts threw this case out of course for various reasons but it wasn't my most comfortable evidence trying to justify the double warning in the washroom not to mention entering the vehicle without a warrant.

* * *

My going to CLEU was obviously a mistake and I couldn't get out. I wanted to do some real police work and have some excitement. My Superintendant at CLEU, Carmen Tough said he would let me go but I would have to find another Detective willing to go there and one that CLEU would accept. I knew already from my past experience that I wasn't that good of a salesman to try and convince another Detective to come here and I may be stuck here forever.

A few weeks later I get called into the Sergeant's office and Bob Murrey tells me he is sorry but they are restructuring the manpower at CLEU and that meant they would have to get rid of one Detective from their unit and that would have to be me. Now I don't think Bob Murrey was crazy about me in the first place because he was the instructor at the Police Academy years ago that told Paul Ballard and his class to be aware of me and some of the other Traffic guys. I told Bob don't be sorry because I have been trying to get out of here for two years and he has just made my day.

The next day I get a phone call at home from Peter Dempster, the Staff Sergeant at the Strike Force office and he tells me they are having some problems between Supervisors and constables and would I be interested in coming back to the Strike Force and do the Road Boss job until the Sergeant is more qualified and experienced. He didn't have to ask me twice. I said I would be there. Peter was one of the five guys that got promoted to Sergeant in 1991 and now he is a Staff Sergeant. I wonder about my decision to file a grievance several years earlier but at least I will be back doing what I do best.

The Second Time Around

In March 1994 I return to the Strike Force for another tour of excitement and I am totally rejuvenated from my first tour after spending 3 years of boredom in the jail and CLEU. I am joined with one of my old Strike Force members, Brad Prentice who was also asked to return to the squad. I was happy about that because Brad was an excellent police officer and he knew what was required for good surveillance.

There was something different though, something had changed in the mere three years I was away. The downtown east side, Hastings Street, also called the Skids, had people openly doing drugs on the street and in the lanes. This area is just beside Gastown, a tourist area and some Police Inspector thought it was more important to have the police presence in Gastown for the tourists than in the Skids where all the crimes were taking place. The drug traffickers took over and the police could never take it back.

There was something different within the Strike Force as well. Naturally all the people I used to work with were gone, transferred to other duties or promoted, God forbid. I had heard that the Constables had been running rough shod over their supervisors in the Strike Force and causing many of them to quit. I could see a different attitude within the squad when I arrived. Now when I was a constable I guess I was a pain in the ass as well but I wasn't telling the bosses what to do and that was what was happening in the Strike Force.

While there are many police members that would like to be doing the Strike Force job, there are only so many that can really do it well. To find a Sergeant or a Detective that can do it well is even more difficult. They are usually older, have more police service and set in their ways and are less inclined to thrive on living on the edge than the younger and newer Constables. Still, you have to have a boss out there, a Sergeant to take responsibility for the squad.

The Strike Force had only been in existence for about 10 years and every year there would be a new course taught by the existing members. If every one that was taught the course from its inception retained 97% of what was initially taught, and the instructors of the day taught their 97% knowledge, the current members would have 74% of the knowledge that was first taught back in 1984. The current members seemed eager but they seemed to think they knew it all. There were certain fundamentals in surveillance but you also had to be flexible and be prepared to change your focus at a moments notice. These new people weren't flexible and they would argue every decision you made at the days end debriefing.

The new Sergeant that I was requested to help was Knute Dalstrom, a big man about 6'4'' and 240 pounds, very easy going but I wouldn't want to get him mad. Knute had been a policeman for 25 years and was being eaten alive by the Constables. In the past years there had been other bosses that the Constables were able to scare off, so this wasn't something new they were doing to Knute. They never gave him a chance.

My job was to be the Road Boss while we were out doing surveillance and Knute was the over all boss other than the surveillance itself. Knute handled it pretty well and did his share of driving and being a foot. At first I think Knute enjoyed the whole change of pace, the surveillance, getting his hands dirty and the different type of work from his previous mundane job as a Patrol Sergeant.

* * *

I had only been back in the squad a short time when it seemed the shit hit the fan. There were homicides occurring involving the Indo Canadian community with gangland style slayings. At first Jim Dosanj was murdered behind a building around 40th and Fraser and then several weeks later his brother Ron is murdered at Kingsway and Fraser as he is driving west through the intersection.

Through intelligence of one sort or another both Squads of the Strike Force are assigned to work on Bhindi Johal, a possible suspect identified by the Major Crime Section. Major Crime wants 24 hour coverage utilizing both Strike Force Squads. My squad was working the 6pm to 6am shift. Every day and night for a week somebody was on him. When he was at home at his parents place on Knight Street we would have someone hiding in a big fir tree on the easement property at the rear of his house near a fenced in BC Hydro area. The lights would always be on at the open rear carport except when some one would arrive at the back of the house. When it appeared that a meeting was going on in the back yard the carport light was turned off. Otherwise the carport light was always on. Everyone would take turns hiding in this tree except for me as I was the Road Boss and in charge. I was lucky. After a week of non stop work and little sleep, the bosses decided to give the Strike Force the weekend off and have CLEU provide the surveillance coverage.

On the Saturday night the CLEU members were drawn away from Bhindis house but they were still close by. They heard some shots from the vicinity of Bhindi's house and on return, found Bhindi's neighbor shot dead in the area of the big fir tree we had been hiding in earlier in the week. The neighbor had taken his dog out for a walk at the back of his house around 2 am and had been gunned down by someone using an AK47.

When I heard about this I called Major Crime and asked if they knew if the carport light was on or off when the first unit arrived after the shooting. I explained if the light was off there may have been a meeting at the rear of Bhindi's house and they may have thought the neighbor was a rival gang member when he took his dog for a walk. They couldn't see the significance and told me if I thought it was important, for me to contact Patrol and ask them. I thought this was a similar attitude from the Detective looking after the Woodward's Store robbery a few years earlier.

One day we are following Bhindi while he is driving his Brother in Laws Nissan Pathfinder east on Highway 91 towards Surrey. We have been able to get the assistance of the CLEU airplane from my old squad member. The plane is a 4 seat Cessna 170 and the pilot says Bhindi is driving so fast he can hardly keep up in the plane and Bhindi is passing cars in the emergency shoulder lane. Knute and I have the speedometer to the very end at 180 km/h. When Bhindi gets to Nordel Way and Brooke Road the engine of the Nissan blows up and he has to stop. We waited and watched his Brother in Law come and get him but that was it for the day.

Surveillance continued over the period of the next month culminating in us arresting Bhindi outside the Gold's Gym on #5 Road in Richmond. Using some flash bangs, (explosive devices) the ERT Squad was called in to arrest him. Bhindi stayed in jail and went to trial perhaps a year later with a hoard of other players.

We are provided with the names of two other players that Major Crime believes did the actual killing of Ron Dosanj at Kingsway and Fraser. These two suspects are not Indo Canadian but Korean and the other Caucasian. We have worked on both for a while and we are in Richmond watching the Caucasian guy. Another white male that looks like a steroid user arrives at this house and he is an associate of and works with the Korean male at a large discount store in Richmond. We are aware of this individual and learn he lives in a rooming house near 5th Avenue and Collingwood in Vancouver. After some time the visiting male opens the front door of the suspect's house, looks around up and down the street, crowing as we call it and walks out to his car with a long 3 foot object, wrapped in paper and wider in the middle. Rob Froese is in the eye and says it looks like it could be a wrapped up AK47 rifle or a very large salmon. It made sense to me because they haven't got anyone for the murder of Bhindi's neighbor and Ron Dosanj was also killed with an AK47. The visiting male looks around a lot before he carefully places this package in the trunk of his car. We start to go mobile and begin following this guy as he is leading us towards Vancouver. I am madly on the cell phone trying to get in touch with Major Crime to see if they want us to take this guy down. I don't want to do it without their knowledge and tip our hand but I think this might be worth it. I speak with one of the lead investigators and relay what we have here but he doesn't seem interested and advises me to just continue following the guy.

We arrive at the guy's house on 5th Avenue and he parks the car and walks up a long flight of stairs and into his rooming house. The guy is observed coming out of the house, crowing around a lot and then returning from the trunk of his car with the 3 foot long package. The guy comes out again still crowing around and removes some small boxes from the trunk that the eye said looked like boxes of ammunition. Again I get on the phone and advise Major Crime and tell them we are about to do a roll over with the other squad and what are their wishes? They will get back to me. The roll over is almost complete when the eye advises that the male suspect has exited the house with a gym bag and something that looks like a long card board roll, like that from Christmas paper, is sticking out of the end of the gym bag possibly covering the barrel of a rifle. The guy drives away. The roll over is completed between the two squads and our squad returns to the office.

When we return to the office Major Crime calls and asks if we would like to get a search warrant for the guy's house. It's a little late I'm afraid. I think the ball was dropped. There isn't much doubt in my mind what it was. I understand it wasn't an easy decision and we didn't want to tip our hand that we were doing surveillance on them but we could have arranged something before the guy got home and at least looked in the trunk. I would have had a patrol car make a routine traffic stop and ask to look in the trunk. If the guy said no, you probably had something and we tip our hand for the murder weapon and get a warrant. It was very frustrating at times because of the job we do in surveillance we see a lot of things that could be helpful in a case but to others it seems unimportant.

Anyway, everyone arrested in the case was found not guilty in court and released. It was later learned that one of the female jurors had been having an affair while the trial was going on with one of the co-accused. Several years later, after continuing to throw his weight around, Bhindi was shot dead on the dance floor of a downtown night club.

* * *

During the surveillance of Bhindi Johal and his crew of thugs, a female member of my squad had been named as a possible target of the gang as revenge from previous police related dealings she had had with them and she was told not to be in the surveillance unit for this file. At the beginning of one of the shifts she stood up and thanked the members for their work and wished she could be with us doing surveillance because it left us with only 9 members instead of 10 and what could she do to help? Jokingly I said while we were gone she could clean the windows and do some vacuuming around the office. Wrong thing to say! Nothing further was said until a month later when I was called into the Staff Sergeant's office. I was advised that this person had gone to someone in the Sexual Offence Squad and complained about my remark and that I may be investigated for Sexual Harassment. I began to stay clear of this person that I proceeded to think was a troublesome bitch. We had had an inter squad baseball game between our two Strike Force squads and one time when this female constable caught a fly ball, one of the guys from the opposing team yelled at her that she was a fucking c--t. I never heard her complain to the guy about his remark so it seemed her problem with me was personal, perhaps that I was brought in to shake up the squad and not about my remarks of cleaning the office.

We are starting to work on more heavy duty crooks and gangsters and the Department decides to give us a little better firepower. We all are given 40 Caliber Barretta pistols and some members are trained on the MP5 rifle. As the Road Boss I had enough responsibilities and didn't need the extra responsibility of handling the MP5.

* * *

There are about four members from each squad at the rifle range practicing with the MP5 while the rest of us are working a day shift B&E file. We are watching a house on 1st Avenue near Victoria and the guy hasn't moved all day. Around 1 pm a car with three guys arrives at the rear of the house and they go inside. About an hour later the back door opens and the same three guys walk down the back steps. I can see our main target from my car and he is talking to the other guys from the top of the porch. He has no shirt on and doesn't look like he is going anywhere soon. As the three get into their car I tell the combined squad that we are going with the car. I have been doing this job long enough and just had a hunch that these guys were up to no good. Within two blocks these guys stop their car and break into a house while the owner, a little old lady is still at home. Everyone is arrested in our usual manner and we return to our office to write our reports and debrief the day.

Where I thought we had a good arrest and we should be feeling good about ourselves I get criticized by this new breed of Strike Force members for leaving our original target and following these guys who we catch doing a crime. The new breed had been trained by someone with perhaps a 57% learning retention rate that you never leave your main target no matter what. I guess they would have sat watching the main guy's house while these other idiots are terrorizing some little old lady two blocks away. Needless to say I was some pissed off. Some of these people have no imagination and are right by the book.

* * *

On another occasion we are working on a Bhindi Johal Associate and this person has made quite a few trips back and forth along Westminster Highway in East Richmond. The road is only two lanes and there are no real parallel streets to use so the Strike Force cars are all in a train behind the suspect. After several trips I tell one of the cars to pass the suspect and go and set up on his residence in case we go there and they can be there and set up when he arrives. Boy, the grumbling I heard that day. "That was outrageous and completely against policy," they said. I told them I was the boss and if I screwed up I would take the responsibility other wise shut up or transfer. I think a couple did transfer.

* * *

We are working day shift and I have just parked my own car at the employee parking lot at Cordova and Columbia and starting to walk towards our office at Main and Cordova. It was Welfare Wednesday yesterday and even though it's 5:30 am there are all kinds of idiots on the streets yelling and screaming and shooting up their drugs. I walk by this rooming house and inside the lobby area I see a set of legs flailing about and I think it is just another one of the over drugged yahoos climbing onto something. I continue walking to the office and I'm the first one there. I unlock the gun cabinet when a couple of the guys walk into the office and say "Hey Grapes, some guy just hanged himself at the rooming house by our parking lot". I sheepishly tell them I think I saw the guy and that I thought he was just one of the idiots.

* * *

A little turf war had been going on between the Russian gang and the Hells Angels. The Russians weren't a big group but they were obviously on steroids and getting in the way of the Hells Angels. There had been one Russian shot and killed a while earlier in front of Trev Deeleys Motor Cycle shop on east Broadway and recently a car bomb went off prematurely on another Russians car near Quebec and Terminal.

We received information about an associate the Hells Angels had hired to complete the hit on the Russians and we were to follow him around. One of the Russian's associates had left his fancy red sports car parked on Quebec and they were too nervous to go and move it in case they would be seen by the Hells Angels or their hit man. The Staff Sergeant asked if I would move it to a safe location. I respectfully declined remembering the last car bomb on the Russian's other vehicle and suggested the Staff Sergeant move it himself if he was so concerned about it.

We followed this hired hit man around driving his 1980 four door Buick for 24 hours a day completing rollovers every day with the other squad. The weekend comes and CLEU is requested to do the surveillance. I learned that their RCMP Sergeant who had a reputation for putting out an anchor on the suspect's car followed too closely and he got heated up. In other words he was following the suspect so close and made turn for turn with the suspect, they say he has put an anchor on the suspect and he is being towed around by the suspect. The squad from CLEU has been doing their surveillance at night and the Sergeant has been driving a blue Chevy Blazer. Because the Sergeant has been heated up, he changes vehicles for the next night's shift and takes out a beige colored Chevy Blazer, same year and model as the blue Blazer. I wouldn't say that showed a lot of imagination.

We have known all along that the hit man probably would have a gun in his car but when CLEU took over the file for the weekend their Inspector was getting nervous about the gun. There is a traffic warrant for the Hit man's arrest and someone has decided to do a traffic stop, arrest the Hit man and have him taken to jail. This is done and the members look inside the trunk of his car and find a loaded Uzi machine gun. Upon instructions from the high command at CLEU , instead of disarming the weapon and covertly making it useless they seize the machine gun and decide to wire the inside of his car for sound. The car is then put into the Vancouver impound lot near Quebec Street.

The Strike Force is back on the file the next day and we are waiting for the Hit man to be released from jail and come and pick up his car at the impound lot. We know the Uzi has been seized by CLEU and there will be some major reaction when the Hit man finds out. We have hearing devices in one of our Strike Force cars to monitor any conversation inside the suspect's vehicle. The guy comes to the lot, opens and closes the trunk, obviously having seen his gun is gone and we follow him out to North Delta and the Panorama Ridge area where he drives into an enclosed garage. The Strike Force members who have the hearing device hear the ripping of the headliner inside the Hit mans car and then no more sound. That was the end of that file.

As it turned out the Russians got killed anyway. One was murdered in Mexico about six months later.

* * *

The daily debriefings have always been a hard time for some members because the new guy always feels picked on. That was one good thing that the old Strike Force boss, Sergeant Bob Thompson was good at, controlling the debriefing sessions. While it may have taken him forever to make a decision out on the road, Bob ran the debriefing sessions well and didn't let things get out of hand. I should have taken more control but I think we had a lot of 74% knowledgeable guys criticizing others for their surveillance miscues. It finally got to Knute and he transferred and went to the Drug Squad.

* * *

Around this time the Strike Force formed a third squad. I wasn't sure that was a good thing or not. Remembering my 74% retention theory, I think we are getting a little thin in real top notch candidates. The problem was we were doing more for Major Crime and less for Patrol or other specialty units and the Strike Force needed more squads in order to fulfill the mandate. I didn't mind doing things for Major Crime but quite often you never heard back from them after you completed a task and you began to feel as if you were just their whipping boy. A case in point is they asked us to follow another Bhindi Johal associate to try and obtain a DNA sample if we can. We are going to have to get some hair or saliva in some way. The associate is a white guy in east Richmond and we follow him around all day and discover he is a smoker. He takes us to the Mylora Golf Course on Sidaway Road in Richmond where he proceeds to pull out a set of golf clubs from the trunk of his car. I get John Geffke out on foot and he goes and talks to the people at the golf maintenance yard. John borrows a set of coveralls, gets a cart and from a distance pretends he is a golf course maintenance crew and follows our suspect around who is playing golf by himself. It didn't take long for the suspect to throw away his cigarette butt or for John to discreetly collect it and bag it for evidence. This took the better part of a day for an eight man surveillance unit and when we turned in the evidence I don't recall a thank you or good job from Major Crime; nothing. Testing for DNA takes a long time so I never did hear the results.

* * *

There were some Constables that were getting quite close to the Staff Sergeant and definitely had his ear. This meant that instead of talking to the Detective or the Sergeant, some were dealing directly with the Staff Sergeant and circumventing the chain of command. I personally didn't like what I was seeing. These were very good officers and I thought friends of mine, but they were getting too manipulative and taking advantage of their good reputations. They got the ear of a newly appointed Deputy Chief and before you knew it the Department was looking at restructuring several ranks after more than one hundred years of Department history.

We got a new Sergeant to replace Knute. Stan Christianson had been a Detective in the Strike Force during my first stint several years earlier only he was on the other squad and he had since been promoted to Sergeant. The other squad in 1989 and 1990 wasn't nearly as rough and as aggressive as our squad had been so we weren't sure how Stan would react to us today. It may have been

five years since Stan last did this type of work so he was expected
to be rusty. I am concerned that the tail is wagging the dog here
and it is time to move on. I decide that I will transfer to the Drug
Squad and work with Knute on the Hard Drug side but I will hang
in at the Strike Force a bit while Stan gets settled in and up to
speed. I continue being the Road Boss for a while and one day
Stan tells me he is ready for the task which is fine with me. Stan
Road bosses for a couple of weeks and he is slow on making some
required quick decisions but that's expected at first. I spoke to him
about it and asked if he thought he was ready even though I am
transferring in about a month. If he's not ready I can stay a little
longer or one of the senior constables like Brad Prentice can take
on the Road Boss duties.

I had tried to stay close to the guys on the squad and take care of
their wishes and concerns about work and safety issues. One night
we are following a B&E suspect and Stan is the Road Boss. The
suspect commits a commercial B&E close to his home and he is
now working his way home on foot. Stan hasn't made a decision
about taking the guy down and everyone is getting pretty anxious
to get him with the goods before he walks inside his house. I told
someone to take him down at Fraser and Kingsway and he was in
custody. Later that night everyone on the squad was coming to me
and saying "Grapes, you have to get the Staff Sergeant to get
someone else to Road Boss". The next day I spoke to the Staff
Sergeant and I told him about the guy's concerns and that I think
they may be right. The next day I went on holidays for a week.

My first day back from my vacation and I return to my desk in the
Strike Force office as the guys are just arriving for work. Stan
calls me into the Boardroom and tells me he was spoken to by
S/Sgt Peter Dempster about the Road Boss issue and he is unhappy
with me and he doesn't trust me. He felt I went behind his back
and I can take the next two weeks off before I go to the Drug
Squad because he doesn't want me around there. I was crushed. I
tried to tell Stan that I had talked to him about making quicker
decisions but I didn't get through to him. Here I am the messenger
who was getting a dressing down for passing on what the squad
felt. I felt terrible that Stan felt that way because I had the utmost

respect for him, but I felt cheated and back stabbed myself that not one of my squad members had the guts to say " Hey Stan, we asked Grapes to say something on our behalf ". I complied with Stan's wishes and at least I showed I was a man and went and shook hands and said goodbye to my gutless subordinates, picked up my uneaten lunch and went home to explain to my family why I'm not working that day. I was too embarrassed and hurt to attend my own going away party as I thought it was too phony to hear all the retirement praises when you just got the shaft. There was definitely a new breed joining the job.

Politics

Police Departments, particularly large Departments, are very political and it can be as dangerous and cruel inside the building as it is out on the streets. Politics was the one thing I didn't like about the Police Department. I understood though and knew how to play the game but unless I believed in what I was selling I didn't want to get involved.

I also had the problem that I couldn't keep my mouth shut and I would tell people what I thought which wasn't always the best thing to do when one was thinking of a career advancement. The structure of the Department is like any other organization, the shape of a Christmas tree with a star on the top, then a few lights near the top, more in the middle and a lot of lights at the bottom of the tree.

When the star, or in our case the Chief, gets replaced, all the lights below are trying to move up the tree and become the top star and all the lights, from the middle of the tree, on up, start clawing for position. Only one light will become the star, but even though you may not have a chance at being the star, you might do well to be on that chosen star's team. There may be six special lights that have a chance of being chosen as the star but which light to align your self with is the big decision. Picking the wrong light could be the end of the upward spiral to your career because it becomes obvious who you are supporting. Sometimes the chosen light isn't even from your tree but brought in from a different tree.

In the mid 1990's the Police Board, who is responsible for hiring the Chief Constable, brought in an outsider, Bruce Chambers from Thunder Bay Ontario. It wasn't a very popular move within the Department and I'm sure in particular for those lights that were near the top of the tree having worked so hard and were so close to promotion but remained unsuccessful. Our new Chief had been the Chief in Thunder Bay which has a similar population as Richmond B.C., a bedroom community of Vancouver. The new Chief was out of his league in Vancouver but I don't think he got a lot of help or support from his Senior Executives either. I was justifiably criticized for the way I handled my disappointment of not being promoted but some of the Senior Executive didn't handle their disappointment much better. The new Chief may have lasted a couple of years before being replaced by someone within the Department.

With the new restructuring of the Police Department the positions of Superintendant, Staff Sergeant and Corporal/Detective would be eliminated through attrition and the last one out is to turn off the lights. The people in the Superintendant and Staff Sergeant positions would be promoted up the ladder in time and just not replaced. The Corporal/Detective rank would be allowed to phase out thereby getting rid of the 'deadwood Detectives' and make room for a new Detective/Constable rank.
(As suspected in later years the Superintendant and Staff Sergeant ranks were brought back after the younger Detective Constables began to get promoted. The Detective rank never returned.)

When the Department started looking in the late 1980's for recruits with at least some University education if not a degree, to do a job that required 95% common sense and 5 % smarts, you knew it might cause a problem. You hire a lot of people that aren't going to be happy being a Constable or a Detective the rest of their career; they want to be Chief. Now we all know there can only be one Chief, so the new people at least want to be near the top of the tree and they don't want to wait for some of the higher lights to burn out by retiring and forcing the new members to wait for years to get promoted. I just didn't think it was healthy to have a lot of back stabbing going on which this system tended to generate.

In a large Police Department like Vancouver with about one thousand members the objective seems to be to get promoted if you want to say you had a successful career. Not everyone wants to or should get promoted and yet the Department has to fill a vacancy and promote someone into the vacant supervisor position. Ideally you would like a leader and not just someone who is in charge and leaders aren't easy to come by.

In 1975 when I was hired, the Department was looking for people who had some life experiences that they could rely on in their role as a police officer. As I previously mentioned in this book, the Department's investigation and background checks of the new recruits was pretty thorough. How much information will be learned on a 24 year old recruit that has four years of university, no job experience and is still living at home with his or her parents? The investigator doesn't have too many people to talk to in his or her investigation. I expressed my thoughts with no success that the married auto mechanic with a grade 12 education, life experiences and a clean life style would have made a better candidate. He probably would be less inclined to be in a rush for promotion and he would be able to relate to the public better than the university graduate. How does a young single, never been married person talk with combatants at a family dispute call when they don't have the life experiences themselves? There is nothing wrong with having a university education as we want the best candidates we can get but I just don't think it should be a pre- requisite of the job like it almost seems to be now.

There was always a little animosity with the Firemen or maybe it was jealously. The Firemen would work a 12 hour shift and if it was afternoons, the perception was that they were sleeping in a quiet hall and then they would leave at the end of their shift and go to their second job perhaps building homes or whatever. The policeman couldn't sleep on the job so he had to go home and go to bed when everyone else was getting up to go to work, that's if he didn't have court that day. The Firemen were always the good guys and were never criticized like the police who had to get their hands dirty with the people. The police always joked that the fireman's motto was 'we fight fires, not people'. Well that was evident at the English Bay riot when the fire got started in the garbage can. The fire department called the police and then got the hell out of there. Never the less, I wouldn't want to do their job unless they made me the ground floor hose man and not have to climb one of those high ladders.

I had a hard time being expected to follow political correctness but I tried to play the game. I got into more trouble talking about police women. My feelings were not different from a lot of the policemen but with my big mouth I voiced my opinion. The women do a great job but are naturally limited when it comes to physical force and I think they get burned out quicker than the men. The women, who are straight, get married, usually, but not always, to a policeman and naturally they wind up having children. Like all of us who have two working parents, the police women has her child care problems as well and wants a steady day shift or office type job. There are only so many of those jobs to go around and that is one less patrol officer on the street. There may also be older more senior police members who have got their hands dirty, taken their lumps on the street and developed a medical condition over the years of work and require that day shift desk job. My wife even disagrees with me about women on the job and she was never a police women. God forbid having two of us running around with a gun.

I was just getting old I guess and becoming the dreaded 'Dinosaur' as so often referred to when someone is past their prime or perceived to be dancing to the beat of a different drum.

You Want Up or Down?

In September 1995 I join the Drug Squad and I am assigned to the hard side of the Drug Section. The hard side is dealing with the heroin and cocaine where the soft side mainly deals with marijuana grow ops. At this particular time crack has not made its way into Vancouver although it is causing a problem in the other major Canadian cities.

When you make a drug buy you are looking for either up, being cocaine, or down being heroin. If you haven't figured it out yet cocaine gives the user an incredible high and feeling of being invincible where heroin makes you very mellow and comfortable.

The hard side is also known as the Street Crew and is made up of ten Vancouver members and ten RCMP members. Vancouver's members are mostly Detectives with a Sergeant and two Constables where the RCMP has one Sergeant; a couple of Corporals and the rest are Constables. Both Forces work together as one unit which is challenging at times but definitely better than CLEU

The RCMP in Vancouver have a huge drug section but most of them work out of 33rd and Heather, 'The Hill', and work on long term projects. They send members to the Street Crew to gain experience at the street level drug scene and I'm sure they also benefit from any intelligence or informants they may garner from there as well. Although I know nothing about drugs I still know my surveillance which is important here and I'm comfortable working with Knute again and I know the other Vancouver members pretty well.

There are certain guys who are good at making drug buys in the skids and I'm not one of them. To be able to make a buy you have to look the part and I'm afraid I'm too healthy looking. The people down on east Hastings aren't your ordinary pot smokers, they are hard drug users and most are pretty gaunt and sad looking. I thought that the Skid Row area was bad when I returned to the Strike Force the second time but it was getting even worse. More and more stores are closing down on Hastings Street because of the drugs and its even beginning to move west of Cambie Street. The Department has put Beat Men on the street again but it may be too late as the traffickers seem to have a good hold of things. Another thing that seems new is there are a lot of Hispanics dealing the drugs now, a nationality that wasn't prevalent in the skids before.

It has been twenty years since I choked out the innocent drug trafficker with Brian McClay on the Granville Mall and here I am ready to do it again. The trouble is there have been changes in the last twenty years in how these people carry their drugs. In the old days they could purchase empty capsules from a drug store and the trafficker would fill the capsule with heroin. Once closed, they would carry it and others in a balloon in the event they had to swallow the balloon and hope the capsules would not dissolve. For a while anyway the drug stores were not permitted to sell the empty capsules to their customers so the traffickers now had to find another method of packaging and distribution. Where can you get an unlimited supply of paper for free, with easy access where you could package your drugs and the powder won't stick to the paper? The answer is Lotto paper from just about every corner grocery store. The drugs are folded very carefully into Points, ¼ grams, ½ grams and so on and the paper is firm making it easy to fold and keep its shape and the drug powder doesn't stick to the paper. The trafficker can't swallow it though if he's checked by the police so they have to develop a new system of distribution. They have a runner, a holder of the drugs and sometimes even a third person holding the money. Now instead of just getting and choking out your man to get the balloon and drugs as evidence, you have three people to contend with. The runner approaches you and asks if you are looking for Up or Down? When you strike a deal and you give the runner your money, he then takes off and meets the person holding the drugs. He gets the drugs and then gives the money to the money man. The runner then returns to you with your drugs in a small flap of Lotto paper. Where a couple of policemen in the past could jump the one trafficker you now need a crew because you have 2 to 3 different people to arrest to get their evidence.

The one problem with the Skids is if you're not selling, you're buying, and if it is night time and you're not doing either, you better be a drunk otherwise you have no business being there and you'll be made as a cop pretty fast. The Department would like us to be in the Skids more often because there is a definite problem there, but you can only make so many drug buys and immediate arrests and then you are burnt. We make the odd buy and arrest in the Skids but most often we try and get the guy to sell higher amounts or at least introduce us to someone who will. Sometimes we make a buy and just record the deal and the evidence and we save him for a drug round up later on in the year.

The Street Crew is supposed to be dealing in low level drug dealers, short term projects, get in and get out and onto someone new. Dial-a-dopers are becoming very popular. They deal in both Up and Down and the user should hope the dealers don't get them mixed up. It is primarily Asians running the Dial-a-Dope operations. The customer makes a phone call day or night and the dealer arrives by car at a specific location and picks the buyer up. The dealer and buyer drive away but the transaction is often completed before they even get to the next block. The customer is out of the car with his drugs and the driver is away with the money. The driver more often than not is not the main man but just a runner making a wage or percentage.

If you know what you are looking for, the Dial-a-Dope operation is not hard to spot. Sit around a pay phone in the right part of town and you will see a drug type make a call and then hang around. A car comes and picks him up and we follow them for the one block car ride. When the customer gets out of the car we have a couple of guys check him for drugs while the rest of the squad follows the dealer in the car to see where he lives, or we don't even bother with the customer out of the car but continue to watch the driver for several days from his house. In either case the aim is to eventually get enough evidence to obtain a search warrant for the dealer's house and car. I can't recall a drug raid on a Dial-a-Doper's house that didn't reveal small children in the house and everyone was on welfare. Welcome to Canada.

When I came to the Drug Squad I brought along some of my learning experiences from the Strike Force such as the baseball bat and its usefulness in getting into vehicles when the driver was reluctant in opening his or her car door. Most of the guys seemed to like this new tool and the RCMP members were willing to give it a try but they seemed to have missed the importance of timing in my original instructions.

* * *

One night we have done our thing and the instruction has come down to arrest this Dial-a-Dope driver. I have the suspect car stopped and the driver will not get out of the car or follow my instructions. I'm at the suspect's driver window that is half way down and I'm leaning inside the car with one hand on the guy's car keys that are still in the ignition and the other hand on the Vietnamese suspect's neck. My face isn't quite inside the car. The RCMP Sergeant, Bert Walton decides this is a good time to try out Barker's bat theory and takes out the drivers side window, missing my head with the bat but still able to blind me with glass shattering all over my face. I said "Bert, are you fucking stupid"? I don't recall his response but he thought it was pretty funny. I had to go to the hospital to get bits of glass washed out of my eyes. I guess Bert never thought of taking out the passenger side window accomplishing the same task without getting me.

We all got along pretty well but I gave the Mounties a hard time and I guess I was pissing off some of their bosses at Headquarters. They were good guys and we were all policemen, but the RCMP training is they are the National Police Force and they seemed to think they were better than everyone else. Some of them might be; but not many. Most are the same as the rest of the police officers, they just have better uniforms. A lot of the RCMP members serve patrol time in small towns and here they are in downtown Vancouver like fish out of water doing foot surveillance in the skids and they all are wearing cowboy boots. One thing you can guarantee is that a Mountie has a pair of cowboy boots and a wedding picture of himself in his Red Serge uniform.

* * *

Word is out that one of my old male classmates from my Academy days and the person who replaced me when I left CLEU has come out of the closet and isn't feeling comfortable in his body. In fact he is feeling so uncomfortable that he is going to have a sex change to become a woman. I was surprised that it was this individual and after all the insensitive laughter had died down I thought, fine it's his business and I guess he will resign and go and be a woman somewhere else, perhaps selling lingerie. I was wrong again. The guy is going to go through all this and remain on the police department only now he'll be a woman. It took a lot of courage to do that but I thought it was the wrong decision to stay on in the Force. In the meantime no-one wants him in their washroom. The guys don't want this person hanging around and the women don't want him in theirs either. The Department has to build him his own washroom because he is the only one of this type on the payroll. There are a lot of insensitive people like me and they are requested to attend a special training day where this individual will explain his life story and how he has been lost as a woman in a man's body for years. My Inspector Ken Dobbs approaches me one day and tells me I should be attending this training class. I tell him there is no way I'm going to listen to this guy describe his woes. I didn't have a training class to tell my woes to when I had twelve liens on my house when our contactor screwed us on home renovations in 1983. That was it, nothing further was said.

After twenty years of service I finally get a free lunch paid for by the Police Department and the City of Vancouver. There are probably one hundred of us that get a twenty year Exemplary Service Medal presented to us at the Stanley Park Pavilion. It was a nice function and our wives who suffered through the past twenty years of our shift work were included for lunch, but only one wife per customer.

* * *

We are doing a drug buy in the skids on east Hastings Street. This area is getting more and more run down with so many of the shops having boarded up windows. We have targeted a specific guy that we believe is trafficking Cocaine out of the Brandiz Hotel bar. Mike Ashton has gone inside the bar as a cover man and we send in our undercover operator to make the buy. When the UC Operator has made the buy he will give the hand signal that the deal has been completed and we can arrest the subject. I have been on the street waiting to hear on the radio if it has occurred but there has been no report. I am wearing a long blonde wig with a head band and a jean jacket and jeans and I look like the overweight father for the band ABBA. As I enter the front door of the establishment there is a long hallway about forty feet from the front door leading to the entry of the bar. I can see the UC Operator talking to the subject and they are partially in the hallway and the bar. I don't know if Ashton can see them. The UC Operator sees me and gives the hand signal that the deal is done and that he has bought the drugs. The UC then leaves the suspect and walks past me down the long hall towards the front door. The suspect then starts to walk towards me as if to exit the bar as well. I have been in both the UC's sight as well as the suspects and have not been able to broadcast that the signal was given and to make the arrest. Instead of letting the suspect exit the bar and losing him, because the guys outside may not be aware the deal has gone down, I decide to take matters in my own hands. I decide to utilize my many years of rugby experience and I will clothesline the guy with my left arm as he goes by and bring him to the ground and arrest him.

As the suspect gets closer I realize he is much bigger than I first thought, but it is too late, I have already begun my cheap shot rugby clothesline move. I put my left forearm around his neck as he is walking by and instead of him bending backwards and falling to the ground as I expected, he is still standing straight up and I have been flung around behind him. I am still hanging on and now I have both arms around the subject realizing I'm in a bit of trouble and no one else knows. I am able to pull the guy to the ground but he falls on top of me and my blonde wig and head band come off. Luckily the UC Operator had not got out the door and turned around and saw what was happening. He came back and while the subject was lying on top of me the UC gave him a good kick to the body. The UC then ran out of the building followed by the subject. I picked up my head band and wig and ran out onto Hastings Street to see a foot chase across to the north side of the street. As I got out to the street my gun fell out of my pant holster onto the sidewalk. I had to stop and come back just as some older black guy was looking at the gun laying there thinking he might claim it. I looked at the black guy as he was looking at my gun on the ground and I told him to fuck off as I picked up my gun and got the hell out of there. All this time I am wishing I had used my right arm for the clothes line move as it was stronger and this would never have happened. The suspect was arrested by the rest of the squad as I was adjusting my hairdo.

* * *

I wore the same wig on another occasion and successfully arrested this low end trafficker in the skids. The Police Station and jail are right in the skids so quite often we just walk our arrested people to the jail if they are semi cooperative. I walk this guy to the jail wearing my shoulder length blonde wig and book him in. The next day we are going down to the skids again and I decide to wear a different wig. Because of my blonde beard my colour selection is limited. I pick out another wig that is more strawberry blonde only a much shorter and more stylish look. I look secretarial as opposed to a cheap one night stand. While I'm not going for the gay look I'm beginning to wonder if that's what I'm portraying with all these wigs. I'm standing on the corner of Main and Hastings acting as a cover person for one of the guys in the process of making a buy. Here comes the guy I arrested last night when I was wearing my other wig and he walks right up to me and asks if he can have some money. He doesn't know who I am so my new wig seems to be working. He is persistent and won't leave me alone continuing to hound me for change. I see the drug deal that I was covering for has safely concluded and our guys are leaving the area. I turn to my bothersome friend and say" Are you stupid or what? I'm the guy that arrested you last night you dumb fuck," and I walked away.

* * *

As the result of several buys from a Dial-a-doper the Drug Squad obtains a search warrant and we do the usual battering ram entry of the suspect's house. Inside are several Vietnamese males, an adult female and a small child. On the dining room table are receipts for their cashed welfare cheques. Each Drug squad member is assigned to a specific room in the house to search for drugs or money and you have to be very thorough which I hated because sometimes I can't find my own socks at home.

A RCMP member was searching the bathroom and he was so thorough that he removed the inset toilet paper dispenser attached to the wall and found a piece of metal clothes hanger hanging down inside the wall that had a bundle of drugs attached at the end. I was impressed.

I was assigned the master bedroom which was a big job. You naturally take the bed apart, mattresses and all. You have to go through everything in the closet and dresser drawers, everything. I find about $7,000 in seven bundles of $100 bills in the dresser and a very expensive men's Rolex watch which I seized as proceeds of crime. I search a baby diaper bag that's on the floor and besides children's clothing it contains about $250 cash and I seize this as well.

Several months have passed and we are in Provincial court and I am on the witness stand. I give my evidence of the property I seized and I explain how the drug money is bundled and then the lawyer for the accused cross examines me. The lawyer isn't happy that I seized this expensive watch from his welfare drug dealing client but he was irate that I went into the baby diaper bag and seized the $250 in small bills and coins and he wanted to know how I justified that. My answer to the lawyer and the judge for the seizure was it was just the beginning of a new $1,000 bundle and every little bit helped. I noticed a few smiles from the gallery in the courtroom but the defense counsel wasn't smiling.

* * *

It's the middle of June 1996 and I'm off again to take the Drug Supervisor's Investigator Course at the Canadian Police College in Ottawa. This is a 2 week course and we are told to bring our hand cuffs, body armor (bullet proof vests) and gloves. I pack everything into my suit case except my handcuffs which I keep in my suit jacket. As I am going through the security screening at the airport I empty my pockets including the handcuffs. Well I'll tell you there were supervisors there in an instant. I showed my badge and said that I was attending a course and needed my handcuffs. They all finally calmed down but the police had been bringing back prisoners for years and I didn't think it would create such a fuss. Remember this was before 9-11. I would probably be shot on sight nowadays.

I arrive at the college and it is the same old place. The whole class is rooming in the old building only this time I have a room to myself with no bible thumping room mate. I wander over to the bar and it's the same old place. I tell you, the RCMP can run a pretty good college.

Ottawa is very hot and muggy at this time of year. You can have a shower but you never seem to dry off. The classmates are from all over the country but most of the students are RCMP with some municipal cops like me from Calgary, Winnipeg and Halifax. There are lots of officers in the country that have never attended the Canadian Police College and I do feel privileged going there, particularly this being my fourth time. The college is pretty much run by the RCMP and they do have the best equipment to train on and money is not spared.

During the course we are going to go into more detail about the drugs and their production, all pretty boring stuff and hard to stay awake when we have all been out partying every night. We do come alive by noon every day as we get into a lot of physical combat. We do a mock entry into a house and I have been chosen to be the squad leader for this exercise. Everyone has their Body Armor and gloves on and the college gives us a helmet with a face shield and a .38 caliber revolver not the .40 caliber I now have at work. The guns are real and loaded with bullets that look like they are made of red wax, like crayons and are the shape of an actual .38 caliber bullet. We do our entry into this vacant house on the College property and we are ambushed by some instructors as we enter the building. There is a lot of yelling and shooting going on and then we debrief the incident. It was fun and a good exercise. We go for a beer and one of the bad guys from the scenario joins us. He tells me he is attending the College for a Traffic Investigator's Course and some instructors asked him if he would help them out being one of the bad guys for this particular exercise. They didn't give him any body armor and one of my guys shot him in the chest. He pulled up his shirt and it looked like he had three nipples with this huge welt right in the middle of his chest. These may not be real bullets but they still hurt.

We watch a lot of movies on Officer Survival and how you may have to fight to the death in some situations in order to survive. We go to the gym and we practice firearm retention. We are on a mat and one guy is trying to get the other guys gun out of his holster. We practice different moves and hand blows to prevent this. I am a month away from my 50th birthday and other than my bad knee, I'm not in bad shape. I lift a lot of weights for exercise but my sparring partner from Halifax is about 38 years old and built like a brick shit house. He is throwing me around like a rag doll but I'm not going to let him know that he's hurting me. My knee was getting sore now and I was happy when the instructor said that was enough, we will save our energy for tomorrow's exercise. I hadn't been thrown around like that since my first wife came after me with a butcher knife. I used the fear and flee method of defense that time and ran out of the house. A week later she came after me with the handle end of a large serving spoon and I thought I could handle that. Without proper training I blocked her lowering blow of the spoon with the palm of my left hand and I was going to give her a right cross with my right hand. The spoon went into the palm of my left hand leaving a big hole and I was on the floor in tears. She started crying because of the week before and what if she had still had the knife. We decided to stop our self defense training then and there.

The next day the class is gathered in the basement of the vacant house and we are all prepared for battle, helmet with a face shield, coveralls, guns, bullet proof vests, pepper spray, leather gloves and all in a 80 degree humid temperature. The only person missing is Lenny from Winnipeg as he was on a similar course a few months earlier. Having a name near the beginning of the alphabet I get to go first. No one knows what to expect and when the scenario is over we are not to return to the remainder of the class to warn them of what is to come. I get to the bottom of the stairs on the main floor and there is this instructor with a clip board in hand and he tells me this is a drug house and me and my squad are doing a room entry and I am doing the upstairs alone.

I slowly start up the stairs with my gun out and at the ready. When I reach the top of the landing there is a door on my left and a door on my right. I slowly open the door on my right and begin to clear the room. You are trying not to make any mistakes because Mr. Clipboard is right there making notes. This room has nothing in it but I check the closet and it's empty. I exit the room and go to the room on the other side of the hallway. I slowly open the door and there is Lenny from Winnipeg dressed in the same protective garb but only he is the bad guy. I start yelling out some commands and Lenny starts walking towards me and he tells me to Fuck Off. I bring out my pepper spray and I hold it too far out from my body and he swats it away from my hand and onto the floor. Lenny is a pretty well built guy about 35 years old and we lifted weights in the gym together and I figure I could be in trouble here. I think back to the gun retention drill where I was tossed around like a rag doll by the guy from Halifax and I decide I don't want any part of that. Stupidly, and for some unknown reason, I throw my own gun out the open door and into the hallway so Lenny can't get it as Lenny and I are now into hand to hand combat. I can see a gun in one corner of the empty room and a large knife in another corner. I am able to throw Lenny to the ground and I lie on top of him holding both his arms to the ground with mine. It is about 11:30 am and it is very hot inside this room. My face shield is starting to fog up and I'm getting tired from the struggle and my heart is starting to pound. Mr. Clipboard is standing over us and I tell him that I am calling for help from the rest of my squad. Mr. Clipboard says, sorry there is no help available. Here I am lying on top of Lenny with his arms pinned to the floor and struggling and our face shields are both fogging up and I'm getting very tired. I think back to the Officer Survival movie and figure I'm not going to lose this fight. I tell Mr. Clipboard once again I'm calling out for help from my imaginary squad. No help available, he says. I don't know what the instructor, Mr. Clipboard wanted or expected to happen but I figure I have no choice. I let go of Lenny's left arm with my right hand and take my right fist and ram it through Lenny's face shield breaking it and cutting Lenny's eye. Mr. Clipboard halts the exercise and tells Lenny to go to the bathroom down the hall and put a cold towel on his face. I feel bad for Lenny but I'm exhausted and glad the exercise is over. Mr. Clipboard says we haven't finished the exercise yet and we should start the exercise over again with him being the bad guy.

Mr. Clipboard is about 35 years old, 5'10", 225 pounds of solid muscle and arms the size of my legs. I figure this guy has been taking some muscle enhancement, stronger than vitamin pills. He is just wearing a T-shirt and blue jeans and no body armor because he wasn't expecting to be involved. I walk out into the hallway and Mr. Clipboard closes the door. I pick up my gun from the hall floor that I discarded earlier and I'm still sucking wind and not ready to start this all over again especially with this guy. I open the door and Mr. Clipboard starts to walk towards me. Fuck it I thought, I haven't got the energy for another fight. I double popped him. I shot him twice in the chest from close range and he barely flinched. At least he wasn't holding his clipboard because I knew he would be making some negative comments. Mr. Clipboard says "That must have been a sympathetic squeeze". I can tell by the look on his face that that's what my answer should be even though I don't know at the time what a sympathetic squeeze is. "Yeh, I guess so", I replied. We do the exercise one more time and he goes very easy on me and it's over I have him handcuffed and in custody. The instructors decide it's time to go for lunch. I apologize to Lenny and when we are at lunch one of the students sees Lenny and his bleeding eye and thinking he was a victim of the instructors, the other student says "This is bullshit. I didn't travel from Surrey to come here and get beat up by these instructors." It was pretty funny. I was glad that I had been wearing my leather gloves otherwise my right hand would have been a mess. I never had the nerve to ask Mr. Clipboard for a look at his bullet wounds and decided to let it go and pretend that it never happened.

* * *

I am back in Vancouver and we have been working a drug file over a year now. In fact we started working this file shortly after I started in the Drug Squad. One of the RCMP members has been buying drugs and working his way up the drug chain for over a year. His nick name at the beginning of the project was 240 Gordie referring to his weight. Gordie is now known as 340 Gordie but doing well on his drug buys. Gordie looks like a Biker with his weight and long shoulder length hair and beard. It is crunch day and Gordie will be buying a Kilo of Cocaine from our suspect, a 66 year old French Canadian that did some serious jail time for shooting and wounding a couple of policemen back east maybe twenty years earlier. We have been making purchases for a while from this guy but not in this amount. Knute used to say in jest that if it wasn't for the RCMP we wouldn't have a drug problem. What he meant jokingly was that we keep buying greater and greater quantities with RCMP money and if it wasn't for us maybe there wouldn't be any dealing going on.

We meet in the office in the morning of the drug buy and take down and go over the plan. Gordie is going to meet Mr. Big in the Fraser Arms Hotel parking lot around 10:30 am. When the deal is done he will give a signal and we'll move in. There is some discussion as to how to move in and arrest the guy. I suggest that a couple of us walk out of the Hotel coffee shop, I will walk by the guy, ask for a light or the time and then smack him and arrest him. I am told thanks Doug for the idea but they want some greater presence. I step back and say OK. It is basically their file and they have spent all this Federal money so they can call the shots on this one.

Well we get down to the Fraser arms and set up. There are no cars at all in the parking lot. We have about seven 2 man cars strategically set up in the area and a helicopter in the air. Gordy arrives in his big Blazer and Mr. Big arrives shortly after in his car. There are now two cars in the whole parking lot, both parked beside each other near the front of the hotel. There is one guy named Barry Tarling who is riding with Al Hutton and Barry is getting pretty edgy. This wasn't unusual because Barry could never stay still and relaxed, he was always on the move driving back and forth past the suspect's house waiting for things to happen. Gordie gives the signal that the deal is done and the order to move in is given. Ross Merritt is driving our car with me as the passenger. As we arrive at the west entrance to the parking lot the scene is like Smokey and the Bandit with some of the cars just about colliding, trying to be the first car there. We are about the third car into the parking lot and I hear a loud bang and think" Oh no, I've seen this before with Doug Lewis in the Strike Force." I look over and I see the passenger side door of Gordie's Blazer open and Barry beside the door with his gun in his hand and a puzzled look on his face. I run over and Barry says "It just went off" referring to the gun he was still holding. There was the suspect slumped over to his right side but still seated. We called for an ambulance and we dragged the guy out and onto the pavement and Knute tried giving CPR but he was dead. There went a year's work down the drain and probably another years worth of overtime in court. It turned out to be the infamous sympathetic squeeze that I had just recently learned about at the

Canadian Police College that caused the gun to go off. When Barry was holding the gun in his left hand he obviously had his finger on the trigger. He opened the car door with his right hand, squeezing the door handle to open it and simultaneously the left hand squeezes as well, causing the gun to fire. The infamous sympathetic squeeze! The suspect was shot through his right upper arm and the bullet went through his arm and into the side of his chest and into his heart. We all went back to the RCMP Headquarters for a Post Traumatic Stress meeting with Mike Webster, a well known police incident counselor. The RCMP told Barry to go on Stress Leave for a month and we never did debrief the actual incident. About six months later, one day before shift I said to Bert the RCMP Sergeant, "Bert, we have never debriefed the incident and talked about what went wrong at the Fraser Arms". Bert said in disbelief "What went wrong? It went like clockwork except for the last thirty seconds". From that I guessed there would be no debriefing, nothing more was ever said about it. I wasn't very happy because this could have been handled my way and nobody would have been seriously hurt but for some reason we needed a big show.

* * *

We split the Drug Squad up for four months while ten of us worked a special project. We rented a penthouse apartment in Burnaby and I went and rented three cars that we could use for making drug buys. Being responsible for renting the cars I took the best one of course, a 1990 white Cadillac Seville. It looked good but it was a bit of a lemon. I would be driving along and then the thing would sputter out on me. This happened several times but I looked good when the tow truck arrived. There was something wrong with the car's computer and I don't think they ever got it right. One of the Vancouver guys used the car one night and made a u-turn in the middle of Broadway and smacked into another car. He returns at the end of the shift and nonchalantly says sorry about that and hands me the car keys. Now it's up to me to straighten it all out with the insurance company and the leasing company.

If the damage to the Cadillac wasn't bad enough I had more bad news thrown at me. We were having our annual Drug Squad party where we honor members who have just been transferred by giving them plaques for their Drug Squad service. I left the Cadillac at home and rode down with one of the other guys because I was going to be the Master of Ceremonies and I knew I would be drinking a lot. The night is getting late and I decide to leave and go home. I get a call the next day that one of the guys from the party had been driving one of my rented cars, left the party and was crossing the Cambie Street Bridge to go home. He ran into a Vancouver Police road block and when he was checked the officer asked him to pull over to the side of the road. The guy did and when the Vancouver member started walking towards him, our Drug Squad member decided to bolt and make a run for it. The car chase is on. Our Drug Squad member takes the 6th Avenue turn off and clips a car at the intersection of Cambie and 6th. The guy continues east on 2nd Avenue with a Vancouver Police Dog member in pursuit. Our Drug Squad guy pulls over at 2nd and Brunswick and tries to make a run for it on foot. The Police Dog takes him down and when the dog handler gets there our guy flashes the Vancouver Officer his RCMP police badge. A little late I would say. The guy was suspended for a year and eventually the RCMP let him stay on because he was a good policeman but he was demoted. Nobody could figure out how this guy could have come up with that decision even when he had been drinking. Now I had another car that I had to return to the car dealer with damage.

* * *

One of the guys I had been working with on the project is a black RCMP member named Jonathon. He was Jonathon, not Jon and very firm about that. Jonathon started out very protective and short with everybody but if you gave him a chance, and even more important if he gave you a chance, he was a real nice guy. He was a good looking guy who was working out and taking Creatine as a muscle enhancer. I was lifting weights so I thought I would give it a try and went and bought some at our local health food store. After about ten days the difference was phenomenal. Not only did my muscles seem bigger but I felt stronger during my workouts.

The trouble was after fourteen days I almost wound up in the hospital with stomach problems that were directly related to the Creatine supplement. There went my chance for muscle beach party.

At the end of our four month project we are now doing the drug round up and arresting all the players that we had bought the drugs from. We have a search warrant for this house and we make a cardinal sin of attempting a double entry. I am at the front door with four other guys and the battering ram and Neil Taylor is at the back door with another four guys and a battering ram. The 'go' is given and we all start trying to gain entry at the same time. Neil and his guys get inside first and once they get in, Barry Tarling, the Nervous Nellie who is back at work from his stress leave, hears us banging at the front door and yells "Shots fired, shots fired." Neil tells Barry to settle down that it is us trying to get in the front door with the other battering ram. As far as I was concerned Barry was far too jumpy for this job considering this and the Fraser Arms incident.

* * *

We are working down in the skids one night and we see a male and female doing some drug trafficking at Pigeon Square, a little park at Hastings and Carrall Street. He has been holding the drugs and she has the money. The park is really a concrete area about 70 feet by 70 feet and it is pretty crowded tonight with a lot of drug types. We get the signal to take them down and I am going to go after the male. I am about eight feet away from him when he looks me straight in the eyes and I realize he has made me. I know I have to get this guy fast or he is going to be gone. I am able to grab him by his collar and we start to wrestle. I pick him up and throw him into a concrete planter box, face first and hand cuff him. It turns out he is Hispanic and has only been here for about six months and already immersed in the drug trade. No big deal, nothing unusual here.

The Hispanic goes to Provincial Court for Trafficking a Narcotic and I am called to the stand. I swear to tell the whole truth and nothing but the truth so help me God. The lawyer for the accused says "Detective, would you tell the court how tall you are and how much you weigh". I have an idea where this guy is going with this and I reply," I'm 5'11" and about 220 pounds your Honor". The defense counsel then says, "Detective, would you tell the court how tall you think my client is and what you think he weighs"? I look at the guy that I threw in the planter box and wish I could make him bigger but I respond " He's about 5'5" and maybe 125 pounds". The defense counsel then says "Do you think it was necessary to throw my client to the ground and arrest him the way you did"? I turned in the witness box and looked at the Judge and said "Your Honor, drugs is a dangerous business and when you put the fear factor in all of us, everyone you are about to arrest looks a lot bigger than they are. I admit the accused looked a lot bigger on the street than he does here today". I felt pretty stupid being made to look like a bully in the court room but that was the lawyer's defense I guess. It can be a nasty business if you play with drugs.

* * *

The Apec Conference (Asia Pacific) is going to be held in Vancouver with President Clinton and Prime Minister Chretien. There will be various meetings at some downtown hotels but the main agenda will be at the University of British Columbia. This is another RCMP responsibility as the National Police Force but they want Vancouver Police assistance. The Drug Squad is advised that we will be doing crowd infiltration because they expect some unrest due to the Chinese leader's attendance at the conference and the Chinese troubles with the Dali Lama and Tibet. A few days before the conference begins we are told to drive around to the various sites and familiarize ourselves with the locations and potential trouble spots.

The first day I am going to be driving around with Jonathon, my black Mountie friend and Darcy Havdale, an attractive Vancouver female constable that we have borrowed from the Vice Squad. First thing that morning Darcy told me that she and her husband, Carl from my Academy class, raise pigs and that her sow had recently given birth. Congratulations Grandma, I thought, but then she proceeded to tell me that one of the babies was not doing well and Darcy thought the baby was starving to death. I listened to Darcy's story with interest but I was a city boy who's only history with livestock was my pet dog. I didn't think Homesteaders got that attached to the animals that they were going to eventually send to slaughter.

It's time to hit the road and the three of us head down to G level of the police underground parking lot. I get into the drivers seat and Jonathon gets into the front passenger seat while Darcy said she will be right with us as she has to go to her own car for a minute. Darcy returns and gets into the back seat of our car and we drive up to the ground level. I look into the rear view mirror and I see Darcy holding a baby pig in this blue baby blanket. No, we won't bring any attention to ourselves I thought. An older white guy with a young black guy and a middle aged female and a baby pig. We exit the parking lot and I think great, four pigs in the car. We drive around and check out Stanley Park and Darcy asks if we can pull over at Brocton Point, a tourist area overlooking the water of Burrard Inlet. We pull over and she gets out of the car, pig, blanket and all and sits down at a bench and starts feeding this baby pig from a baby bottle. Jonathon and I both had a laugh but how far is this going to go? At the end of the day I told Darcy leave that God Damned pig at home tomorrow.

The rest of the conference went pretty well. I got right into the crowd infiltration role and participated in demonstrations and marches with the usual chants, "Hey, hey, Ho-Ho, the USA has got to go" and all the usual anti government chants. I even got my own sign that said 'Free Tibet'. One night the demonstrators were gathering around this flag pole at UBC that was a significant location and they were demonstrating because one of their main agitators had got himself arrested earlier in the day. It's raining out and I have the hood of my rain coat up and a ball cap and some yahoo is climbing up the flag pole. All the agitators circle around the flag pole, hold hands and start singing Kumbaya. I look around and I see the RCMP riot squad suiting up with their face shields and batons. I am holding hands with an RCMP female on my right and the guy to my left asks why I am here, because I look too old to be a student. I told him my daughter was a student at UBC and I'm supporting her cause, but I thought fuck you telling me I look too old. The RCMP are now starting to bang their shields with the batons and I think there is nothing more these guys would like to do than to take a round out of me. I make up some excuse and get the hell out of there before there is bloodshed, namely mine.

The next day is the expected big riot and I have drawn a front row seat, sitting in our unmarked car with Knute inside the fenced area where all the rioters want to get to. I know we have several squads of armed Crowd Control Units hidden in the buildings. There are snipers on all the roof tops and many uniformed members armed with large containers of pepper spray protecting the temporarily constructed fences. There are maybe a couple of thousand demonstrators and they make a run for the fence causing it to sway over a bit. I think this is going to be good as Knute and I are eating our lunch in the front seat of the car and couldn't get involved because we are in plain clothes. The demonstrators made a couple of attempts but the pepper spray fended most of them off. We don't get a show but Ross Merritt participating in a 'sit-in' on Marine Drive when the RCMP Staff Sergeant known as Sergeant Pepper, sprays the crowd with a big huge fire extinguisher full of pepper spray. The dignitaries all got away safe and sound and there weren't any serious injuries. Fun was had by, if not all, at least a few of us.

I had had enough of drugs and was ready to move on to something else. The nice thing about being a Detective was the ability to move around to different jobs if you wanted and not stay at the same old job. My old buddy Dave Bromwell from Team 31 was now the Sergeant in charge of the Vice Intelligence Unit and Bob Delf Jr. from CLEU and I both put in for a transfer to this unit.

Sex, Sex, Sex

It's the fall of 1997 and Bob Delf Jr. and I are starting our new careers in the Vice Unit. At one time the Vice unit dealt with gambling and liquor as well as prostitution but now it is sex, sex and more sex. I am going to learn that there are all kinds of vices out there as well as a lot of very sick and deranged people.

Prostitution is the oldest trade in the book and it's nothing new to the City of Vancouver, but it has become more out in the open than in the past. When I was in my early 20's and even when I joined the job in 1975 there weren't the hookers out on the street like they are today. I think one of the biggest reasons for the change was around 1976 when a Vancouver Police Inspector had it in for The Penthouse Night Club and its owner, Joe Philiponi. The Penthouse Night Club had all the ladies of the evening inside the club as patrons and the gentlemen would go to the club, pick up a date and then leave with her. Later, after completing their business, the same lady would return alone to the Penthouse and the nightclub would charge her another $5 cover charge or entry fee. The Police Department, after a long undercover operation, considered this and some liquor offences to constitute the running of a Bawdy House and raided the club. The club was closed for sometime before reopening after a lengthy trial. Incidentally, the owner, Joe Philiponi was murdered at the club a few years later. The ladies of the evening now had no where to ply their trade except on the street.

The temporary closing of the Penthouse created a new and bigger problem for the city officials. Instead of having all the hookers working indoors and out of one location we now have them standing on the street corners and becoming an eyesore and a nuisance to many citizens. There were a couple of different groups of girls and some started hanging out on Davie Street while some others got more dressed up and looked a little classier hanging out at Georgia and Hornby Street. The Police Department would chase them off from one area but they would eventually appear somewhere else. In time they moved to an area that the Police Department was satisfied with and while the police still went after them for prostitution, they didn't seem to try and chase them away with the same effort any more.

For some years the police went after the girls by tricking them. That is to say an undercover police officer would pretend to be a customer and obtain the required evidence to charge the girl with prostitution. Like every other type of case, the lawyers get involved and some became specialists in defending the women. The undercover officer would have to get the hooker to say what she was going to give him, be it a blow job or a lay and how much it was going to cost. The more times the girl has been arrested and gone to court, the smarter she became in the legal process. It was really an exercise in futility. The lawyers were making lots of money defending the girls. The cops were making lots of money going to court. The girls were working twice as hard to pay for their lawyers and the City was paying large overtime cheques for the cops. Somewhere along the line it was decided to stop arresting them and turn a blind eye but keep track of them and get the young girls under 18 years of age off the street.

Now, in 1997 there is a general area for each type of sex trade worker. The high end girls are working the club district, Richards, Nelson, Helmcken and Seymour Streets. These girls were a lot harder to trick (arrest) because they had been around and understood what evidence was required to charge them. They would only say so much on the street and you had to go to a hotel by taxi and then finish the negotiations with them inside the room.

There was the Kiddie Stroll where a lot of the juvenile girls hung out, mostly at night time. This was an industrial area around Victoria and Franklin Street and we concentrated on this area. We would try and discourage the girls from working and we would take their photos for our records in the event something happened to them. If they wouldn't leave and they were juveniles, we would trick them in order that they would have to go to court and have a Judge impose some restrictions on them keeping them from prostitution. At the very least we went after the customers called the Johns.

There was the Transvestite area around Clarke and Hastings and Boys Town down around Drake and Hamilton. I'm sorry but I never tried to trick one of the boys myself. Then there were the real sad cases around the skids, Hastings and Main where the girls were so addicted to drugs, they were aged beyond their years and would do just about anything for $5.

Add to all this and you had a flourishing inside trade that worked out of high end establishments to low end dives that were passing themselves off as legitimate massage parlors.

If you didn't want to deal with a real live human being, what about a video? We have men and men, men and boys, men and women, women and women, urination, fellatio and what about animals. What is a vice? What is normal? Does anybody really care? Vices are like discussing marijuana. Everyone has an opinion about it and many people think they are victimless crimes and should be legalized. The problem is what is an acceptable norm?

* * *

There were only eight people working in the Vice Unit and there were a lot of vices out there. Bob and I partnered up and while we assisted everyone else with the girls on the street, we took a keen interest on the inside workers at the massage parlors. We started out looking at an establishment that was located in a building at Hornby and Dunsmuir. This was a first class operation that had operated for 25 years and for some reason had a business licence issued by City Hall. The first time Bob and I went there we got off the elevator and as we walked into the lobby on the fifth floor, a group of beautiful women wearing baby doll outfits and high spiked heels appeared from around the corner wearing huge greeting smiles. I would say "relax girls, we're just the cops. We need to see some identification". The ladies would then go stomping off to get their purses and the boss, Misty, a beautiful lady herself, perhaps in her 40's, came out from her office. We explained not only who we were but also that we were there to ensure there were no juveniles working there. Misty was very cooperative and showed us around the place. There were about 8 different rooms and each had a different theme. One room had a huge round bed and another had a dance floor with the usual brass fire pole to the ceiling. There was a mirrored room and a shower room and so on. A customer would be charged a fee for a massage and the fee varied based on which room the customer chose. Once inside the room with the lovely Barbie doll of his choosing, the customer would be offered sex for an additional fee. This would be considered an agreement between two consenting adults in a private place. This upscale establishment and its owner would say they knew nothing about it and only charged a fee for the room. It is a big game, but it is a whore house. Both Bob and I thought the girls were a lot safer working in there though than on the street.

The next top rated massage parlor was located near Richards and Nelson and was partly owned by Misty and another lady named Veronica. It wasn't the same scale as the Misty's business but it was also pretty well run. We would make the same entrance and I would make the same announcement to the loosely clad ladies of the evening. I was writing the girls name in my note book and as we always did with anyone we took information from and I asked this particular girl for her address as well. That didn't sit well with Veronica and we got off to a bad start. She didn't think that the girl should have to give me her address and I see what her concern was. Maybe I was a crooked cop or wanting to hustle her employee later. That wasn't the case and I tried to explain that to Veronica. I told her I thought this was a whore house and we are investigating the employees and we need information for follow up contact. Veronica put on the offended look and told me it wasn't a whore house that it was a legitimate massage parlor. We left it at that.

About a month later Bob and I are cruising the Kiddie Stroll late one night and we see a girl working alone and we pull up and talk to her. During the conversation Bob asks her why she doesn't work inside at a massage parlor where it might be safer. The girl, who was in fact an adult, said she had worked for Veronica at her establishment on Richards. I asked why she left there and she said she didn't get along with Veronica and that Veronica had a manual for teaching the new girls the sex trade and would demonstrate giving a blow job using a banana as a prop. We went and saw Veronica immediately after that and I told her about the banana story. She admitted that the business was a whore house and we got along fine after that.

* * *

Both Misty's and Veronica's businesses were classy places and also in a commercial environment. There were maybe hundreds of girls advertising in the newspapers or the internet but were performing their services out of regular homes or apartment buildings.

Bob is the good looking guy in our partnership but he makes me do the phoning to the prostitutes and making the appointment to be serviced. We would get into the suite and most often the girl didn't even live there but just used it as a whore house. We would call the manager of the building and have her ass kicked out of there and caused some inconvenience I guess, but it wasn't fair to have her there among regular tenants.

There were lots of places that advertised as massage parlors and Bob and I would check them out to see who was working there and if it was really a massage parlor or just a front for a whore house.

There were a couple of places we went into that were located in commercial areas and the owners said they had been there for 20 years and we were the first policemen that had ever been there.

It seemed like the whole thing was just a game. The city in fact licensed girls to be escorts. Every Tuesday and Thursday the Vice members would have to interview girls at the police station who had applied for an escort license. We would take their picture and ask them if they knew what they were getting into and how they planned to do their business. The trouble was I don't think the City Licensing Department knew what it was getting into or what the hell an escort did. Some of the girls were up front and said what we already knew; that they were going to be inside hookers. Others would try and pull the wool over your eyes and say they were just a companion for an executive on a date. I would say to the girl "see my partner there, he's a good looking guy, right?" Of course they all responded that he was. Then I would say "why the hell would he pay $200 for hockey tickets to take you to a hockey game and then another $200 to take you to dinner and then another $200 for your company when he could get some girl from a bar to join him for free"? Finally the girl would agree that she is going to be a hooker.

* * *

You never knew who you might run into around the stroll. Until somebody actually stops, picks a girl up and leaves the area, the driver of the car could say they were just driving by to have a look at the girls. They could stop and say they were asking for the time or directions or they just wanted to get the girl off the street themselves. One dayshift Bob is driving our car and I see someone that I think I recognize having met them at a party and they are talking to a black sex trade worker at Franklin and Salsbury Street. I run the cars plate and sure enough they are someone my wife and I knew casually. The girl gets in the car and they drive away. Bob had to make a u-turn and we got stuck in traffic so they got away. I just thought it would be interesting to stop the car and see how it played out.

* * *

Bob and I being rookies in the squad were pretty naïve to begin with on how the whole sex trade worked. It's the winter time and quite cool outside. We are driving down Hastings Street near Clark and we see a beautiful blonde standing on the corner wearing a blue bikini bathing suit and exposing a huge set of breasts. Bob tells me to turn around and we'll get a picture of her. We took pictures of the prostitutes on the street for our Vice Unit computer records. I pull up beside the female about 30 years of age and Bob suggests she get out of the cold and get in the back seat. We start talking about her business and the subject of her breasts comes up. She tells us that they are the new saline breasts and she had the older silicone breast replaced. That was all very interesting but was more interesting was when she showed us her identification and her name was Raymond. We took Raymond's photo and told everyone back at the office and they all knew about him so we felt a little stupid. Raymond looked a lot better than our transvestite policeman.

We tried to discourage all the girls from working on the street but particularly the young ones. They had all the answers though, not to worry. The girls would say "I have a spotter to take down the licence plate of the cars I get into". Not many did. The spotter most often was their pimp and I never saw them taking down any plate numbers. The girl gets into a stranger' car in the middle of the night and takes the customer to a secluded dark location to perform a sex act. Who knew that she got into the car? The girl goes missing and how long is it before someone notices? Some of the girls move around between Calgary, Edmonton, Vancouver and Las Vegas. It is a tough business to be in unless you're the pimp.

* * *

Not everything happened on the street or in a massage parlor. We received word from an anonymous source that a mother was interested in making some money by allowing her 5 year old daughter to dress up in seductive clothing and be fondled by a male customer. While it seemed impossible that someone would do this and the information might be false, we thought we should look into it in case it was true. I drew the short straw and phoned the mother and arranged to meet her at a coffee establishment at 64th and Granville Street, a location close to where she lived. We had coffee outside on the patio while the rest of the squad was nearby in case any arrest was to be made. It wasn't easy pretending to be a pervert and interested in children but the mother was pretty careful about what she said and what the child would do. The mother never got angry at the suggestion of such an activity but we never arranged a final deal and nothing came out of it. The original information wasn't that reliable but where there's smoke there's fire. I just don't think she trusted me.

There was no shortage of people who liked children, particularly on the internet where they thought they could protect their identity. The internet investigations were just starting to come about, at least at our Vancouver Department. We had a member, Detective Bruce Heathrow, that wasn't attached to the Vice Unit but was a computer geek and he started coming across this stuff.

Through the internet Bruce had come across a guy that was looking to have sex with a small child. Using a false identity, Bruce helped to make arrangements for one of our female members to pretend she was a mother willing to allow her small child to partake in a sexual activity and meet the guy at a local hamburger restaurant on Hastings Street in Burnaby. We had arranged for a room at a hotel across the street and we had a couple of guys waiting there. Bob and I were in the restaurant covering the meeting and in comes this well dressed business man about 60 years old carrying a brief case. Besides the money he was going to pay, he brought along some new toys that he bought for the child to play with. The deal was made and the suspect and undercover policewoman went to the hotel room where the young child was to be staying. Unfortunately for the suspect there was no child, only the cover team that arrested the guy. To me this is sick. At least with a guy doing a violent crime you feel justified in being a little rough when making the arrest but here you are just dumbfounded at the way this man's mind worked. We ended up executing a search warrant for his house and we seized his computer for evidence. He was a well respected businessman in his community in the out skirts of Vancouver and had a nice wife and family.

We had a similar kind of incident only Bob and I received the information from one of the girls that ran an inside massage parlor. There are hundreds of women who are living in apartments in the west end and Yale Town that are running mini massage parlors or whore houses. Our major concern was they were operating in public buildings where people lived and we didn't think this should be happening there so we started harassing them. In order to get us off her back, this girl gave us this information about the body guard of a very famous actress who was in town and making a movie. The male body guard had contacted our prostitute and enquired about having sex with a child around 10 years old. The film crew was staying at the Pacific Palisades Hotel on Robson Street so we arranged to have our undercover policewoman pose as the mother and meet the guy at a coffee shop at Robson and Bute Street. We used the same police woman as before and a guy about 35 years old arrives. The deal was done and we arrested him on the street. The guy was American and had $1500 cash on him. We advised the film crew about the arrest and he was immediately fired and the Crown seized his money and deported him the next morning. I don't know that he ever returned for court. I doubt it.

* * *

It was time for a break from the pedophiles and maybe just deal with the regular johns. Bob and I are watching this one girl about 10 pm and see her get picked up by a guy using an auto body courtesy car. We follow the car and it pulls into an underground parking lot and I tell Bob to park in the lane and give them a minute. After about three minutes we walk down into the parking lot with our flashlights and interrupt this 70 year old man getting a blow job from this horribly sick looking prostitute. It turns out he had just dropped his wife off at the Church Bingo and decided he needed a little entertainment as well. We laughed pretty hard. What a sight. They deserved each other.

* * *

While the practice of tricking the girls had stopped, we did it on occasion if she was a juvenile and wouldn't get off the street. That was the only way we could get conditions from the court and more help for the kid. I am the john and drive an undercover car up to our young prostitute. When I have obtained all the evidence the arrest team will stop us, arrest her and we can do the same to another girl without me revealing my true identity. The young prostitute and I go through the usual greeting and she asks if I am looking for company. I tell her I am and she gets into my car. I start slowly driving and ask her how much will it cost. She asks if I'm a Cop and of course I say no. She tells me the cost is $60 and I have to ask her what I will get for that and she tells me a blow job. I have the evidence and start lightly touching the brake pedal so the arrest team behind me will see my flashing tail lights and know the deal is complete and stop us and arrest her. The girl is telling me to turn here and then to turn there and I keep pumping my brakes for the arrest team to stop us. The girl is starting to rub my leg and I wonder if the arrest team is just playing with me because I see them behind me. Finally they put on their red light and pull us over and eventually arrest her. It was a good thing because I didn't have $60 on me.

* * *

I was kind of missing the real action and one day Bob and I are parked down on Great Northern Way eating a takeout meal. It was the summer time and it was still light out and maybe 7 pm. The emergency alarm goes off on the radio that there has been a double shooting around 8th Ave and St. George Street. Bob is driving the car this day and I suggest we head up there. Bob looks at me as if I am crazy and says "we don't want to go there". I said yes we do, but I think I had got Bob into too many predicaments already and he thought I was suicidal. I got him to head up there but we could have walked faster than he drove. There were all kinds of Patrol cars there but I wanted to look for the guy but Bob's heart wasn't in it. I guess Bob was remembering the botched car take down and the arrest at the ferry terminal when we were in CLEU and didn't want to go through that again.

* * *

We had an additional police women assigned to our unit and she was a real looker. I thought she was a dead ringer for Pamela Anderson in every way but maybe not as smart. Her name was Sylvia Armstrong and we started using her as bait to catch and arrest the Johns out on the Kiddie Stroll. Sylvia arrives at work wearing this very tight outfit with a zip up top. We have several cars keeping an eye on her and Bob and I have taken out a van so she has a place to rest and warm up from the cold street. We throw her out on the street and about forty minutes goes by and we haven't got any bites yet; just a bunch of looky loos. We get Sylvia back in the van and suggest she zip down her top half way and then put her back on the street. In no time we are arresting guys and we get her back in the van. Sylvia says the last guy was weird. "He wanted to put his thing between my boobs and do it that way" she said. I told her that was called a tit fuck and she said "Oh is that what it is". Sylvia was the best UC operator for a call girl we ever had. Unfortunately there was more to the job than standing on the street corner, looking good and pretending to be a whore. You had to get involved in the investigations as well.

* * *

The Vice Unit is still sharing some office space with the soft and hard side of the Drug Squad. One night Sylvia and her junior partner have arrested a 14 year old girl on the Kiddie Stroll and brought the juvenile back to the police station for an interview. They are questioning the young girl in the Detective Lounge when a Drug Squad Detective walks in the room with a 24 pack of canned beer. The Detective places the beer in the fridge for the end of their shift and he tells Sylvia and her partner they can have a beer if they want to and the Detective leaves the room. Sylvia cracks open a beer for herself, her partner and one for the 14 year old girl. Sylvia's partner took the kid's beer away and they finished the report and interview. The next day Sylvia was transferred to a different department.

* * *

We never had enough people in the Vice Unit to do the things we wanted and we all had different areas of interest and expertise. While Bob and I were getting pretty knowledgeable about the inside prostitution scene we still would help out with our John stings out on the street. The Vice Unit had taken on two very junior constables with about five years police experience. These two guys were university graduates, looked like twin fire plugs, about 5'9" and 170 pounds and they had come up with some new computer scheme for managing all the prostitutes in the city. It was supposed to be a temporary position but to their credit they had the bosses right up to the Chief, buffaloed with this program. These guys got to fly everywhere around the world. I thought it was the biggest scam but they were getting away with it. The Twins, as we called them, would occasionally help out on the stroll with the arresting of the Johns if they weren't busy giving a lecture someplace. One time I watched them arrest this straight looking guy for trying to pick up a hooker and they had him pushed up against a wall and were working him over. I told them to calm down and I advised the Sergeant when we got back to the office. You know by now I don't mind a little violence, but this isn't a bank robber or a B&E guy. This is a guy that was cooperating after being arrested but had tried to pick up a prostitute and was being charged for it. I thought to myself if they didn't have a badge or a gun they wouldn't be doing this because they would have got hurt. As I said, 95% common sense and 5% smarts.

* * *

My left knee, in particular my ACL has started to give me a lot of problems to the point where I book off sick and I go to my family Doctor. He arranges for me to see a specialist but he tells me I should have fought the Workers Compensation decision back in 1985. I begin an appeal process with WCB and request that they send me a copy of the original operative report from the surgeon who fixed my MCL ligament after my rugby injury in 1977. I get a copy of the 1977 report and the surgeon notes at the time that other than my MCL, the rest of my knee including my ACL was fine. It turns out WCB had this report when they denied my claim in 1985 and still stated my ACL damage was all part of my old rugby injury.

After pointing out the 1977 medical report and my belief that they were in error in denying my 1984 claim WCB reopens my claim and I have arthroscopic surgery where I have arthritis throughout my left knee.

I attend the WCB physio clinic in Richmond B.C. for several weeks and instead of building wishing wells, this time I am actually having physiotherapy. A representative from WCB attends at my work place with me, my Sergeant, a member from Staff Development and a lady from the City's Risk Management Section. Workers Compensation has said that I may be entitled to a disability pension if I'm unable to perform my police duties and this meeting is to discuss the duties and activities of my job. At the present time while I am off work WCB is paying the majority of my salary but if they can get me back to work on light duties, the Police Department will have to pay the majority. We have our little meeting and later that night the WCB member calls me at home and says the Police Department advises there are no light duty jobs for a Detective and the WCB member says the Department is playing" hard ball". With the Police Department saying this, that there are no light duty jobs, they are able to have the majority of my salary continuing to be paid by WCB.

I am advised ten days later by WCB that they have denied my claim once again and I am on my own. The City and the Police Department are now paying my salary while I am off work and not WCB. I am starting to feel depressed about the whole situation as this injury has now gone on for sixteen years. I get a phone call at home from the Police Staff Development Section, the same fellow who had said there were no light duty jobs for Detectives, and he has the gall to ask me if I can come back to work on light duties. I went crazy to say the least. I felt I was being used as a pawn between the Police Department and WCB to see who would get stuck paying me. I couldn't sleep at night. I dreamt crazy ideas of wearing fatigues and taking over the WCB building and taking out the Vancouver Police Staff Development officer as well. As time went on it got worse and they said I had a nervous breakdown. I didn't think I had but I just wanted to hurt some assholes that had ruined my life. What added insult to injury was a year earlier Detective Constable Barry Phips had been in the United States on a case and got in trouble with drugs and prostitution which resulted in a major investigation back in Vancouver by our Internal Investigation Unit. Barry wasn't fired for his behavior but allowed to use up his sick time for several years and then retire with his pension. I thought I deserved a little more support from the Department than Barry Phips got. I just wanted to be treated fairly, I wasn't looking to be on long time sick leave or retire.

My wife and I go and see the Police Department's Doctor who happened to be my family Doctor for twenty years before he accepted the Medical Officer position with the City and he was my family Doctor through my work related injury in 1984. He prescribed some "happy pills" as I called them and we went home and came back a week later. The Doctor asked my wife how I was doing and how are the pills working? She replied that I was much quieter now but I just sat in the chair and had drool running down the corner of my mouth. The Doctor lowered the dosage and I could then function normally. I was still off work but I was getting better and I had lost the urge to be Rambo which was a good thing.

I got a phone call from Wayne Meyers, the Inspector in charge of the Vice Unit and my old Sergeant and friend from the Strike Force Days. He asked me if I would come back to work as the Acting Sergeant in charge of the Vice Section because the current Sergeant had taken ill and when he was better he would be going to the gambling section. I had been off work long enough and I wasn't making any headway with WCB so I would try going back.

* * *

I return to work and find my partner Bob Delf is off on long term sickness and probably will not be back. I start doing my Sergeant duties which includes being on the road with the squad members as well as attending a lot of daytime meetings. It's just not the same.

The twins who were only to be here on loan, are still doing their lecture thing all over the country and feeding their egos leaving only six other people to do a pretty massive job. I tried to get the bosses to transfer one of the twins and have the other twin train another member in their program but the bosses would have none of my suggestion. Rowland was pretty good but I thought Omar was a lazy slug and was always off sick. There was no real camaraderie among the group as they all had different interests and it was a different time I guess. A few days before Christmas I got permission from my Inspector to take everyone out for dinner and buy a few drinks instead of their regular shift for the hard work they had all done. We go to the nearby watering hole the last shift before the holiday and I buy a round of drinks and about an hour later ask who wants another because I am dying of thirst. No one wanted another drink, they had had enough. Wow, what a lively group I thought. I could see retirement may not be too far away as this is going to be pretty painful.

I submitted a brief report suggesting the City and the Police Department send me to Amsterdam to meet their authorities and discuss their prostitution and Bawdy Houses in order to determine if it would be worthwhile implementing in Vancouver. I thought what the hell, the City and the Police Department aren't doing much to discourage prostitution now and a better system might be safer. There were no bursts of laughter but I never went on the trip either. It's like legalizing certain drugs, no one wants to discuss the topic because it's too complex.

* * *

There was a street worker's advocate, Janet Hanlon who had got the attention of the media and was regularly on open line radio talk shows promoting safer sites for prostitutes to work from and calling down the police. I didn't disagree with a lot that she was saying but she was promoting her house as a safe place where the women could go to and ply their trade and she would supply the condoms and what ever else was needed like creams and gels. We all know the inside sex trade is a game and that the Department closed its eyes and lets not talk about it. But this woman is openly embarrassing the Department as if to challenge the police to do something about it. As I'm the Sergeant in charge I'm instructed by my superiors to look into the situation.

I arrange to have Detective Neil Taylor and a police woman, posing as a prostitute, go to Ms. Hanlon's house and get a room for some sexual activity. From previous experience in the Drug Squad I'm not going to have Neil drive any cars that belong to our squad lest they get damaged. Neil and the under cover policewoman go to Ms. Hanlon's house where she personally greets them at the front door and they are provided with a room to have sex. Everything goes fine and they get the evidence we need to support a charge of keeping a Bawdy house. We don't do anything with the charges at the time because the Department is still reluctant to create a can of worms and just wishes the woman would shut up and get off the radio.

A day or two later we are working the afternoon shift and being the summer time it's still light out. I am sitting in my office doing paper work and one of my people tells me to turn on the radio. The radio talk show host, David Berner, is telling his audience that in the next hour his guest will be none other than Janet Hanlon to discuss the prostitution business and her safe house. That's it. I tell a couple of my members that we are heading up to her house and we will arrest her for the Bawdy House charges when she comes out to go to the radio studio. We set up and a taxi arrives at the house and sure enough Janet comes out and walks toward the cab. Now, Janet is about 6'2" and 250 pounds with long shoulder length hair and wearing a dress. I could tell that Janet from her voice on the radio might not be the woman she is posing as and I'm sure of it when I can barely get my handcuffs around her large wrists. At this point Janet starts yelling in a high pitched voice that she is having a heart attack. The neighbors are now coming out of their houses and I tell the cab to get lost and I call for an emergency ambulance even though I suspect this act is a complete charade. The ambulance arrives and I send one of my members in the ambulance and the other to follow it to the hospital. I return to the office to start my notes.

I am putting pen to paper and turn on the radio and the talk show host is apologizing to his audience because his guest, Janet Hanlon is late for the show and they will have to move on to another topic. I guess the radio host got word what had happened and the radio people started calling the office and wanted to know what was going on. At the same time I'm trying to arrange for someone from Patrol to guard Janet at the hospital so my two officers can return to the office and complete their reports. The hospital has given Janet a clean bill of health but think she should remain in the hospital over night. In order to not have to have a police guard with her all night which is a requirement as she is under arrest and a police prisoner, we decide to issue her an appearance notice where she promises to turn herself into the front counter at the police station the next day and my two members can return to the office.

The following day Janet arrives at the front counter as promised but as expected there is a throng of media cameras there as well. We whisk Janet out the side door and over to the new jail by the Remand Centre across the street from the police station and arrange to have her booked in. When the Sherriff is filling out the booking sheet they ask what sex Janet Hanlon is so they know whether to put her in with the men or the ladies. She is still in her very nice dress and I say I think she is a male but what if I'm wrong and she is just a very large ugly woman. The female Sherriff takes Janet to a private room and the Sherriff returns and advises me Janet is a Transvestite with the hose still attached. I thought to myself, I think I've had enough.

I have been the Acting Sergeant for almost a year now and I'm beginning to think maybe it was a good thing I didn't get promoted to Sergeant ten years earlier because this isn't much fun. It might have been different at a different time and place, like Traffic, but it's too late now. I'm too crippled to ride the bikes anymore and it's too late to transfer now. I have a desk job and I miss the excitement of being on the street and the world of the unknown or what is going to happen next. I'm now 54 years old and I have 26 years on the job and I can retire without a penalty.

On June 1, 2001 I turn in my badge and gun, say my farewells and walk out the door.

The Aftermath

Sir Robert Peel (1788-1850) helped create the modern concept of the Police Force in England and one of his main principles was the police are the public and the public are the police. The public, or people, do stupid things in their lives and the police being part of the public are no different, they have their turn at doing stupid things as well.

As you have read in this book, I have had my share of doing stupid things in my career as a policeman. There were times that I acted inappropriately or I should have got a search warrant and didn't. I am not asking for acceptance for my actions but they happened. They happen every day in other careers as well, whether you be a Judge, a lawyer, a Doctor or Dentist, a Priest or Minister, a politician or even a media celebrity. These other career screw ups just aren't as publicized as when the police screw up.

You have to have thick skin to be a policeman and unfortunately not many of us do. You are expected to be brave, tough, strong and most important honest. You are expected to be sincere and sensitive and have no biases. You are expected to have a college degree of some kind and yet be worldly and have common sense. You are expected to be squeaky clean and yet operate in a world filled with grey matter. You are expected to make the correct decision at all times even though many of the decisions are made at a fraction of a second. When you make a mistake, and you will, you hope it is a small mistake and not a life ending decision. Show me a street cop who has never made a mistake and I'll show you a cop who has never done anything. If you make a questionable call the smarter people of the world will chastise you. The Talk Show hosts who earn a very healthy six figure income and their overly intelligent listeners, the first time callers but long time listeners who don't seem to work but are available to call in at 10 in the morning, to share their opinion on the decision you had to make at a moments notice. That instant decision may have been made with fear and adrenalin running through your veins. After the media and the public have had at you, then you are subjected to a defense counsel who wants to embarrass and shame you on the witness stand in court. The defense has had the pleasure of obtaining all your notes and that of the crown's case so he or she can look for a loophole to attack your evidence and get their client off. That is the system and you live with it.

Police officers actually are a very critical group and will criticize themselves when one of their own screws up and policemen don't like crooked cops. There can be thousands of dollars just sitting there in front of you or millions of dollars worth of drugs at a drug raid to tempt a crooked cop. There are horror stories of cops who have stolen drugs or money or even personal items from people. The police will take care of that person themselves; they don't need uninformed, inexperienced outsiders doing it for them. A policeman earns a fair income with a lot of deductions. A Police Officer doesn't have many tax deductions and you contribute dearly to the pension fund. There is no Christmas bonus, no free turkey and no Christmas party. If you are lucky enough to even have Christmas off, you can have a Christmas party but you pay for it yourself. When you go for coffee or lunch at a restaurant you may be approached by someone who wants to complain about a traffic ticket they received by someone other than you and you have to politely listen to them vent as you are eating your meal. You may get an emergency call and have to leave your lunch. You still have to pay for it. Many officers quit or think of quitting police work between 7 and 10 years of service. If you get past that and make it to retirement, the pension is good. You however made a large contribution to the pension, not just the city. Many tax payers think your pension is all paid for by the city and that is not so.

All that being said, it is a good job. Like any job it's what you make of it. I just don't know if they are having fun anymore. You have to have a sense of humor or you could go crazy. There are so many sad and depressing things that you see when you work the streets and if you don't see the funny side of life at times you will go nuts. I see some officers taking themselves far too seriously as if they are going to save the world. When that happens I think the thought of common sense can go out the window. Police work is still 95% common sense and 5% smarts.

It concerns me that as a result of many coroner's inquests over the past 33 years we have continually received new and improved weapons to address the various threat levels the officer may face and yet sometimes the easiest weapon is chosen and maybe not the appropriate one. We have come a long way from the old .38 caliber Smith & Wesson revolver with the round nose bullets to the 40 Caliber Barretta, the ASP and the Taser.

I have never used the Taser as it wasn't around for police work when I was a police officer. The Taser or something similar had been around even in the 1970's but it was a prohibited weapon for anyone to have at that time and it was sometimes in the hands of the criminals. I am sure the Taser under the right circumstances is a good option to deadly force, the last and final force option. I worry that an officer is going to the Taser too quickly without trying the other force options of talking, physical force or even the pepper spray. I have seen several incidents televised on the news where the Taser was deployed and they all seemed to be gratuitous or over the top in my opinion where there were four or five officers present who should have been able to handle the situation by other means. There were two incidents where some elderly people, while not being overly cooperative but not threatening, were Tasered by a lone officer.

As a result of the past 33years of inquests, the police have been authorized to carry metal batons (Asp), OC or Pepper Spray and a large Kel-light flashlight. These tools seemed to have gone by the wayside for the faster and perhaps less physically demanding Taser. I am not suggesting that a police officer should expect to get beat up every time he or she goes to work, but the very nature of the job has a danger and risk factor to it. I don't think we can just zap someone because they aren't complying with our every command.

Sometimes the best solution is to temporarily back off from the situation until help can arrive. When I took the drug course in Ottawa in 1996 we saw a training video of a Police Officer in the southern States stop a car with three Hispanic men in it. This video which is the officer's own police car camera has been seen on local television as well. The police officer is a big man, about 6'5" and is at the back of the suspect's car with the trunk open. There is a duffle bag in the trunk and the officer smells marijuana and starts questioning the driver and wants him to open the bag. There are three guys in the car and the officer is alone on the highway at night and he only has one set of handcuffs. A second guy exits the car and walks to the back and joins the first suspect and the Officer. The two suspects start talking in Spanish and they overpower the policeman to the ground. The third suspect exits the car and one of them shoots the policeman with his own gun killing the policeman. Then they drive away. Hind sight is always 20/20 but after getting suspicious about the duffle bag I probably would have said, "On your way" to the first guy, let them drive away and follow from a distance and requested back up. Life is very short and sometimes losing an arrest isn't the biggest thing in the world. Hell, he only had one set of handcuffs and even if he had a spare set he was still short of a set because of the third guy.

When you start thinking of using a high level of force like your gun or a Taser you have to consider are you alone or are there two, three or four of you? Is the situation that important or dangerous that you have to use a high level of force and can you justify it? If you can, fine, but sometimes we are going to have to get our uniforms dirty and sustain a scratch or a cut. I am lucky in that I never had to fire a shot on duty in 26 years but I did get dirty and had a few scratches. I honestly believe that Police Forces need to develop some kind of courage test for recruits applying for that type of work. That's not to say you have to be Bruce Lee or John Wayne but at least have a little gumption to stick your nose into a situation and not be afraid to get it bloodied. I was far from the toughest guy around but you had to have some confidence in yourself and not pull out your gun or Taser at every tough situation. If you are timid as a policeman and always relying on your gun or the Taser to back yourself up, then the chances are pretty good that you're going to use that weapon because once you have reached that level of force, you can't go back. When that gun comes out of the holster there are only two options left. Putting your finger on the trigger and then pulling it or putting the gun back in the very stiff front break holster which is not easy to do these days without taking your eyes off the suspect. Remember Barry Tarling in the Drug Squad and the Fraser Arms incident. If the gun didn't come out nothing would have happened.

If you have to fire your gun you have to shoot at the body mass and not the arm or the leg as many civilians suggest. You are under extreme stress and could miss the arm or leg and hit an innocent bystander and you are still in danger from the suspect you are dealing with. It has been proven that a person armed with a knife could attack and stab an unsuspecting officer from 30 feet before the officer could get his weapon out and fire a shot.

In police circles there is the old saying "It's better to be tried by twelve than carried by six". It's better to be alive and tried by a twelve man jury than dead and carried by six pallbearers. This is still true but its hell to be criticized by the public and your peers, for an action that you took that may not have been necessary.

It is a lot busier now than in 1975 and even 2001 when I retired. There are a lot more guns on the street that the police have to worry about and a lot more gang activity. But the average criminal is the same and the crazy's are still crazy. The family disputes haven't changed and a drunk is still a drunk

My advise to a new police officer is be careful out there and try and have some fun along the way because it's a long career. Try and laugh at your funny mistakes, and you will make them, because everyone else is laughing at them but be an honest cop more than anything else.

At the end of your police career you will have some good stories to tell; stories that the insurance agent will never have.

It has been one hell of a ride and I miss it.

THE END

Made in the USA
Charleston, SC
22 March 2012